The Urban Gardener

From Balconies to Indoor Rooms to Back Yards - Cultivating Lush Spaces in Urban Places

Thomas Finch

The Urban Gardener

© Thomas Finch All Rights Reserved 2023

**The moral right of the author has been asserted
First published by Rockwood Publishing 2023**

All rights reserved. This book contains material protected under International and Federal Copyright Laws and Treaties.
Any unauthorized reprint or use of this material is strictly prohibited.

This book or parts thereof may not be reproduced in any form, stored in any information storage/retrieval system, or transmitted in any form by any means – electronic, mechanical, photocopy, recording, or otherwise – without prior and express written permission from the author and/or publisher.

Copyrighted © 2023

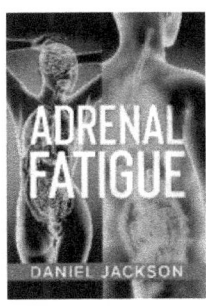   

Take a look at more great books available from Rockwood Publishing

... **some for FREE!**

Just visit the link below:

rockwoodpublishing.co.uk

Contents

Chapter 1: Introduction to Urban Gardening and Sustainable Living 1

What is Urban Gardening? 1

The Importance of Sustainable Living 3

Benefits of Urban Gardening 6

The Rise of Urban Gardening 9

Chapter 2: Getting Started with Urban Gardening 12

Understanding Your Space 12

Equipment Essentials for Urban Gardening 14

Assessing Sunlight, Water, and Weather Conditions 20

Chapter 3: Selecting the Right Plants for Urban Gardening 28

Native Plants and Their Benefits 28

Easy-to-Grow Vegetables and Herbs 31

Best Plants for Small Spaces and Urban Environments 33

Ornamental vs. Edible: Balancing Aesthetics and Function 36

Seasonal Considerations 39

Chapter 4: Techniques for Maximizing Small Spaces 42

Vertical Gardening: Growing Upwards 42

Container Gardening: Flexibility and Convenience .. 47

Hydroponics: Gardening without Soil 51

Window Gardening: Making Use of Natural Light ... 56

Chapter 5: Soil Management and Composting 59

The Importance of Healthy Soil 59

Soil Testing and Amendments 64

Understanding Soil Types and pH 67

The Importance of Composting 69

Natural Fertilizers 72

Chapter 6: Natural Pest Control and Plant Care 75

Common Pests in Urban Gardens and How to Control Them 75

Plant Care: Watering, Pruning, and Fertilizing 80

Planting and Care for Edible Gardens 83

Planting and Care for Ornamental Gardens 86

Seasonal Care for Your Urban Garden 89

Chapter 7: Setting up and Maintaining Different Types of Urban Gardens 92

Designing an Edible Garden 92

Designing Your Garden Layout 97

Creating an Ornamental Garden 99

Developing a Wildlife-Friendly Garden 101

Attracting Beneficial Insects 104

Creating a Bird-Friendly Garden 106

Building a Miniature Wildlife Pond 108

Chapter 8: Sustainable Living Beyond the Garden...111

Reducing Waste: Plastic-Free Gardening and Composting 111

Water Conservation: Rainwater Harvesting and Efficient Watering 116

Supporting Local Food Systems: Community Gardens and Farmers' Markets 119

Reducing Waste in Your Garden 121

    Chapter 9: Case Studies and Success Stories 125

Inspiring Examples of Urban Gardens Around the World 125

Interviews with Successful Urban Gardeners 128

Lessons Learned and Tips for Success 130

Best Practices for Harvesting...................................132

Preserving and Storing Your Produce 134

Enjoying Your Harvest: Simple Recipes and Ideas .137

    Chapter 10: Moving Forward: Expanding Your Urban Garden 141

Taking Your Urban Garden to the Next Level.......... 141

Engaging the Community in Urban Gardening 146

Urban Gardening and Its Impact on Mental and Physical Health 149

Experimenting with New Plants 152

Advanced Hydroponics and Aquaponics 155

Joining Urban Gardening Communities 157
  Chapter 11: Conclusion: The Future of Urban Gardening and Sustainable Living 161

The Role of Urban Gardening in Sustainable Cities 161

The Growing Trend of Urban Farming 166

Lessons from Urban Gardening Experts 172

How Urban Gardening is Changing Cities 177

Final Thoughts 183

Chapter 1: Introduction to Urban Gardening and Sustainable Living

What is Urban Gardening?

Urban gardening is an innovative and transformative practice, a testament to human adaptability and our yearning to connect with nature, even within the confines of concrete jungles. It is the art and science of growing plants in an urban environment, where space is often limited, and conditions might be less than ideal for conventional gardening.

For those who live in cities and densely populated areas, urban gardening opens up a whole new world, offering an escape from the hustle and bustle of city life, a chance to grow your own food, and a sanctuary that fosters mental wellbeing. But urban gardening isn't just about green spaces and fresh produce; it's a lifestyle choice that promotes sustainability and community-building.

So, what exactly does urban gardening look like? It can take many forms, from window-sill herb gardens and balcony tomato plants to rooftop gardens and community allotments. It could even be a wall covered in lush, verdant greenery or a small aquaponics system in your kitchen. The beauty of urban gardening is its versatility and accessibility, offering anyone, regardless of their living situation, the opportunity to get their hands dirty and experience the joy of nurturing life.

As our cities continue to grow, so do the challenges we face. Pollution, food insecurity, the loss of biodiversity, and the disconnection from nature are all significant issues. Urban gardening offers a hands-on approach to tackling these problems, providing a pathway towards a more sustainable and balanced urban lifestyle.

But how does urban gardening contribute to sustainability? Well, growing your own food reduces the demand for commercially grown produce, which often involves extensive transportation and harmful farming practices, thereby reducing your carbon footprint.

Gardens also act as carbon sinks, absorbing carbon dioxide from the atmosphere. Additionally, gardens can help manage stormwater runoff, provide habitat for local wildlife, and even help cool cities during hot weather, reducing the need for air conditioning.

Moreover, urban gardening fosters a sense of community. Shared garden spaces can bring people together, encourage cooperation, and create a sense of belonging. It's a rewarding endeavor that not only improves the physical landscape of our cities but also the social fabric, nurturing relationships among neighbors and promoting a culture of care and responsibility for our shared spaces.

With the right knowledge and techniques, anyone can become an urban gardener. This book aims to guide you on that journey, offering practical advice and insights drawn from years of experience and scientific research. We'll delve into the different types of urban gardens, the best plants to grow, strategies for dealing with limited space, tips on organic pest management, ways to maximize yield, and much more.

Urban gardening is more than a hobby. It's a powerful tool for change, a movement towards a greener, healthier, and more connected society. It's about taking control of our food, our health, and our cities, one plant at a time.

So, whether you're an experienced gardener looking to adapt your skills to the urban environment, or a complete novice with a desire to learn, there's never been a better time to dig in and get started.

Welcome to the world of urban gardening. Let's grow together."

The Importance of Sustainable Living

Living sustainably means making choices that meet our current needs without compromising the ability of future generations to meet theirs. It's about acknowledging the interconnectedness of all things and recognizing that the decisions we make today have far-reaching implications for tomorrow.

In the context of our modern world, where resources are dwindling and the health of our planet is increasingly under threat, the need for sustainable living has never been more apparent.

We're living in an era of climate change, biodiversity loss, and escalating social inequality. These challenges are formidable, but not insurmountable. By embracing sustainability in our daily lives, we can each contribute to the solutions.

So why is sustainable living so important?

Firstly, sustainable living helps conserve resources. Our planet's resources are finite, and we're consuming them at an alarming rate. Water scarcity, deforestation, and soil degradation are just a few examples of the consequences of our overconsumption. By living sustainably, we can reduce our consumption, waste less, and make more efficient use of resources, ensuring they're available for future generations.

Secondly, sustainable living can significantly reduce our environmental impact. From the carbon emissions of our cars to the plastic waste generated by our throwaway culture, our daily activities contribute to pollution and climate change.

By choosing to live sustainably, we can minimize our environmental footprint, protect ecosystems, and combat climate change.

Thirdly, sustainable living promotes social equity. Sustainability isn't just about the environment; it's also about people. It's about ensuring everyone has access to the resources they need, not just now, but in the future. By embracing fair trade, supporting local businesses, and advocating for social justice, we can promote a more equitable and inclusive society.

Lastly, sustainable living can improve our health and wellbeing. By eating locally grown, organic food, reducing our exposure to toxins, and spending time in nature, we can enhance our physical health. Moreover, living sustainably can give our lives a sense of purpose and fulfillment, knowing that our actions are contributing to a better world.

So how does urban gardening fit into all this? Urban gardening is a tangible, enjoyable way of practicing sustainable living. It allows us to grow our own food, reducing our reliance on the industrial food system and its associated environmental impact. It reconnects us with nature, promotes biodiversity, and provides a space for relaxation and mindfulness.

Above all, urban gardening is about community. It's about coming together to create something beautiful, nourishing, and sustainable. It's about learning from each other, sharing our successes and failures, and growing not just plants, but relationships.

We're going to explore in greater detail how to create an urban garden, the role it can play in sustainable living, and how you can use it to make a positive impact on your life and your community.

It's an exciting journey, and we're thrilled to be embarking on it with you. Let's cultivate a better future, one garden at a time.

Benefits of Urban Gardening

Urban gardening, while seemingly a humble endeavor, is a powerful instrument for change that extends benefits beyond the beauty of greenery and the joy of harvesting your own produce. Let's explore some of the significant ways urban gardening can enhance your life, your community, and your environment.

1. **Food Security and Nutrition:** Urban gardening can play a pivotal role in addressing food security concerns in cities. By growing your own fruits, vegetables, and herbs, you can have direct access to fresh, nutritious food. This is particularly beneficial in urban "food deserts," where access to fresh produce may be limited.

2. **Physical Health:** Gardening is a physically engaging activity, offering a wholesome form of exercise that can

contribute to overall fitness. Whether it's digging, planting, weeding, or harvesting, the activities involved in gardening can enhance muscle strength, flexibility, and endurance.

3. **Mental Wellbeing:** Urban gardening can have profound effects on mental health. The act of nurturing plants, being outdoors, and physically connecting with the earth can reduce stress, anxiety, and depression. It can provide a tranquil oasis in the heart of the city, offering a space for mindfulness and relaxation.

4. **Environmental Impact:** Urban gardens help combat climate change in several ways. They absorb carbon dioxide, helping to offset urban carbon emissions. They can reduce urban heat islands by cooling their surroundings. Moreover, they contribute to stormwater management, decreasing the likelihood of floods during heavy rains.

5. **Biodiversity:** Despite being in an urban environment, gardens can support a wide range of life. They can provide habitats for insects, birds, and other urban wildlife, contributing to the city's biodiversity. Planting a variety of crops can also promote genetic diversity, an essential component of overall biodiversity.

6. **Education and Engagement:** Urban gardening provides a hands-on opportunity to learn about nature, food production, and sustainability. This makes it an excellent tool for engaging children and adults alike, fostering environmental stewardship from a young age.

7. **Community Building:** Shared gardening spaces, like community gardens or allotments, foster social interaction and community engagement. They can become places where people gather, share knowledge, and work together towards a common goal, thus strengthening community bonds.

8. **Economic Savings:** Growing your own produce can lead to significant savings over time. It allows you to cut back on grocery bills, particularly if you're growing high-yield and high-value crops. Plus, it reduces the costs associated with food transportation and packaging.

9. **Waste Reduction:** Urban gardening encourages waste reduction and recycling. Composting kitchen scraps turns waste into valuable, nutrient-rich compost for your garden, reducing the need for synthetic fertilizers and the amount of waste sent to the landfill.

10. **Aesthetics:** Last but not least, urban gardens add beauty to the cityscape. They can transform drab, grey spaces into lush, green sanctuaries, improving the aesthetics of the neighborhood and increasing property values.

The ripple effect of these benefits is extensive. They interconnect, amplifying the impact of urban gardening on a personal and societal level. In the following chapters, we will delve deeper into these benefits and provide practical guidance on how to realize them in your own urban garden.

The Rise of Urban Gardening

Urban gardening, though not a new concept, has seen a remarkable resurgence in recent years. The reasons behind this resurgence are many, reflecting the diverse benefits urban gardening brings to our cities, communities, and individual lives.

The growth of urban populations has played a significant role in this trend. As more people move to cities, the demand for green space and locally grown food has increased.

However, the available space for traditional gardens is limited. This has led to innovative solutions, like rooftop gardens, vertical gardens, and container gardening, allowing urban dwellers to cultivate plants in whatever space they have available.

Increasing awareness of environmental issues and the importance of sustainability has also contributed to the rise of urban gardening. Many people are becoming more conscious of their carbon footprint and looking for ways to live more sustainably. Urban gardening provides a way to reduce this footprint, by decreasing reliance on commercially grown produce and its associated transportation and packaging waste.

Food security is another driving factor. The realization that our food system is fragile and susceptible to disruptions has led many people to take control of their food supply. Urban gardening offers a way to do this, providing access to fresh, nutritious food and reducing dependence on supermarkets.

The community-building potential of urban gardening has also contributed to its popularity. In our increasingly digital and isolated world, community gardens offer a space for social interaction, cooperation, and a sense of belonging. They can also serve as educational spaces, where children and adults alike can learn about nature, food production, and sustainability.

Finally, the mental and physical health benefits of gardening have gained recognition, especially in the wake of the COVID-19 pandemic. As people sought ways to cope with stress, anxiety, and the challenges of lockdown, many turned to gardening. The therapeutic benefits of nurturing plants, combined with the satisfaction of growing your own food, have made urban gardening an appealing pastime for many.

It's clear that the rise of urban gardening is more than a passing trend. It's a response to the challenges and opportunities of urban living, a testament to our adaptability, and a powerful tool for creating more sustainable, resilient, and connected communities.

As we continue to navigate the complexities of the 21st century, it's likely that urban gardening will play an increasingly important role in our cities and our lives.

In the next chapters, we'll delve into the practicalities of urban gardening, from choosing the right plants and making the most of your space, to dealing with common challenges and maximizing your yield.

Whether you're a seasoned gardener or a complete beginner, we hope this book will inspire you to join the urban gardening movement and experience the many benefits it has to offer.

Chapter 2: Getting Started with Urban Gardening

Understanding Your Space

As we embark on this journey into the verdant world of urban gardening, the first step is to truly understand and appreciate the space that you have. While your available gardening area might seem restrictive or limiting at first, remember that even the most compact spaces can be transformed into thriving green oases.

Urban environments offer a unique set of challenges, but also a wealth of opportunities. From balcony gardens to rooftop greenery, vertical walls to window sill planters, urban gardening is all about making the most of the space you have. So, let's start by getting to know your gardening space and its potential.

The first thing to consider is the size of your space. Measure the area accurately and note down the dimensions. This will help you decide what kinds of plants you can grow, and how many. Small spaces can benefit from vertical gardening methods, while larger areas might accommodate raised beds or even small trees.

Next, observe the amount of sunlight your space receives throughout the day. Sunlight is crucial for photosynthesis, the process by which plants convert light into energy. Most vegetables and flowering plants require a good amount of sunlight, generally at least 6 hours a day. However, there are also many shade-tolerant plants if your space doesn't get much sun. Try to notice when and where the sunlight hits, as this will influence where you place certain plants.

Consider, too, the direction your garden faces. South-facing gardens generally receive the most sunlight, while north-facing gardens may be shadier. East-facing gardens enjoy morning sun, perfect for plants that prefer cooler conditions, while west-facing spaces get the afternoon sun, ideal for plants that thrive in warmer temperatures.

Also, take into account the wind exposure of your space. High winds can damage plants and dry out soil, but some spots might be shielded by walls or buildings. If wind is a concern, think about incorporating windbreaks such as trellises or taller, sturdy plants.

Another key factor is understanding the nature of your soil. Different plants have different soil needs, and urban soil can often be compacted or contaminated. You might want to consider getting your soil tested for nutrient content and potential pollutants. If the soil is poor, don't despair. It's always possible to improve it with compost or to use containers filled with store-bought potting mix.

Also, think about access to water. Plants need regular watering, and it can be a challenge to lug watering cans up several flights of stairs or across a large rooftop. Consider how you'll get water to your plants, whether through a hose, watering cans, or an automatic irrigation system.

Lastly, consider your lifestyle and how much time you can commit to your garden. Some plants require more care than others. If you're a busy urbanite, you might prefer low-maintenance plants or ones that can thrive with a bit of neglect.

As we delve further into the world of urban gardening, we'll explore these concepts in greater depth. For now, start observing and thinking about your gardening space with these considerations in mind. Remember, understanding your space is the first crucial step towards creating a flourishing urban garden. The process of discovery and adaptation is as rewarding as the eventual lush growth you'll nurture in your city home. Let's move forward, one plant at a time, turning grey to green and creating urban jungles in our living spaces.

Equipment Essentials for Urban Gardening

Urban gardening is a brilliant way to go green, eat fresh, and even reduce your carbon footprint. But to get started, there are some essential tools and equipment you will need to get your city garden flourishing.

Let's start with the basics.

1. Hand Tools:

No matter the size of your garden, you need to have the right tools on hand. Here's a short list of the essentials:

- **Trowel**: This is your go-to tool for planting, digging small holes, or breaking up clumps of soil. Look for a sturdy one-piece design, and don't forget to clean it after every use.
- **Pruners**: A good pair of pruners is indispensable for maintaining your plants. Choose bypass pruners for their clean cuts which help plants recover quickly from pruning.
- **Garden Gloves**: A durable pair of gloves will protect your hands from thorns, sharp tools, and soil.
- **Watering Can or Hose**: Depending on the size of your urban garden, you'll need a suitable watering system. For small balcony gardens, a watering can might suffice, while larger rooftop gardens might require a hose with different spray options.

2. Containers:

Urban gardening often means container gardening, as soil-based plots are scarce in city environments. Here's what you should consider:

- **Size**: The size of the container should match the plant. Small pots are perfect for herbs and small

flowering plants, while larger ones are needed for vegetables and big flowering plants.
- **Material**: Containers come in various materials - plastic, terracotta, metal, or ceramic. Each material has its own set of advantages and disadvantages. For instance, plastic retains moisture well but may not be as aesthetically pleasing as terracotta or ceramic.
- **Drainage**: Ensure your container has good drainage to prevent waterlogged roots, which can lead to root rot, a common plant killer.

3. Soil and Compost:
A good quality potting mix is essential for urban gardening. It provides the right structure for roots to grow and holds the necessary moisture and nutrients.

- **Potting Soil**: Choose a high-quality potting mix suitable for your plants. It should be light, well-draining, and rich in organic matter.
- **Compost**: Composting is an excellent way to recycle kitchen waste into rich, nutrient-dense soil. Many compact compost bins are available on the market that fit perfectly in small urban spaces.

4. Vertical Gardening Systems:
In the context of urban gardening, you may need to think vertically. Vertical gardening systems, like trellises, wall planters, and hanging baskets, are great ways to utilize space effectively.

5. Lighting and Temperature Control:
Depending on your location, you may need to consider equipment for lighting and temperature control.

- **Grow Lights**: If your space doesn't receive enough natural sunlight, grow lights can supplement or replace natural light.
- **Shade Cloth**: Conversely, if your garden is in an area that gets too much sun, a shade cloth can protect your plants from getting scorched.
- **Heaters/Coolers**: In harsh climates, heaters or coolers can help maintain optimal temperatures for your plants.

6. Seed Starting Supplies:
Growing your plants from seeds can be a gratifying process. Here's what you'll need:

- **Seed Trays**: These trays are perfect for starting your seeds. They often come with a clear lid to create a mini greenhouse effect, which encourages germination.
- **Seed Starting Mix**: This is a light and fluffy soil mix that provides your seeds with the optimal conditions for germination.
- **Labels and Marker**: These are essential for keeping track of what you've planted. It's easy to forget, especially when you're dealing with a large variety of plants.

7. Fertilizers and Pest Control:

Maintaining the health of your plants also requires the right fertilizers and pest control measures.

- **Fertilizers**: Organic fertilizers, such as fish emulsion, seaweed extract, or worm castings, provide essential nutrients to your plants.
- **Pest Control**: Natural pest control methods are best for urban gardens. Consider introducing beneficial insects, using insecticidal soaps, or creating DIY traps for common pests.

8. Garden Cart or Organizer:

As your tool collection grows, keeping them organized and portable becomes crucial. A small garden cart or tool organizer can help you transport your tools with ease and keep them in one place.

9. Plant Supports:

For certain plants, especially climbing ones or those with heavy fruits, plant supports are necessary. These can be in the form of stakes, cages, or trellises.

10. Measuring Tools:

When it comes to gardening, measurements matter. Here are a few handy tools:

- **Rain Gauge**: This tool helps you keep track of rainfall, crucial for adjusting your watering schedule.

- **Soil pH Tester**: Different plants prefer different pH levels. A soil pH tester can help you maintain the ideal pH for your plants.
- **Thermometer**: A thermometer can help you monitor the temperature of your garden, especially if it's indoors or in a greenhouse.

11. A Garden Journal:
While not a physical tool, a garden journal is a must-have. Recording your plantings, observations, successes, and challenges can provide a wealth of knowledge over time. It's a place where learning from experience transforms into wisdom.

Urban gardening is more than a pastime; it's a way of life. It's about creating an intimate connection with nature, right in the heart of the city. With these tools and equipment, you're well on your way to creating your own urban oasis.

Enjoy the journey, relish in the challenges, and take pride in every bit of green you add to the concrete jungle. Every plant you nurture is a testament to life's resilience and a tribute to the harmonious coexistence of nature and urban life.

As you embark on your urban gardening journey, remember that the best garden is one that brings you joy. It's about more than just producing fruits, vegetables, or beautiful flowers. It's about the satisfaction of nurturing life, the thrill of seeing your plants grow and thrive, and the serenity that comes from being connected to nature, even in the heart of the city.

There's a certain magic in gardening, and urban gardening is no exception. It's a world where tiny seeds become lush, green plants, where small spaces become vibrant oases, and where city dwellers become urban farmers, cultivating not just plants, but also a deeper appreciation for nature and for life itself.

So, gather your tools and roll up your sleeves. It's time to dig in and start your urban gardening adventure. The beauty of it all is that you're not alone on this journey. This book, as well as a whole community of urban gardeners, is here to guide and support you every step of the way.

Assessing Sunlight, Water, and Weather Conditions

Urban gardening, the practice of growing plants and food in city environments, has been steadily rising in popularity. As more city dwellers become aware of their ability to cultivate their own fresh produce in small spaces, the urban landscape is gradually transforming into a mosaic of greenery.

But before we delve into the nuances of seed selection, soil preparation, and pest control, we must first focus on the fundamental parameters that can make or break your gardening endeavor: sunlight, water, and weather conditions. This chapter will guide you through the process of assessing these factors, ensuring you're well-prepared to embark on your urban gardening journey.

The Role of Sunlight in Urban Gardening

In the world of plants, sunlight is the equivalent of our daily bread. Sunlight provides the energy plants need to perform photosynthesis, a process that converts light energy into chemical energy, feeding the plant and enabling it to grow.

Most fruiting plants, such as tomatoes and peppers, require at least 6 to 8 hours of direct sunlight per day. Leafy vegetables, like spinach and lettuce, can tolerate some shade but still need a good 4 to 6 hours of sunlight.

In an urban environment, sunlight availability can be a bit of a challenge due to tall buildings and other structures that can cast long shadows. You will need to observe the pattern of sunlight and shade in your potential garden space throughout the day and across different seasons. Take note of any structures or objects that could block the sunlight at different times of the day.

Remember that the sun's path changes with the seasons, so it's essential to evaluate your space throughout the year to get a comprehensive understanding.

If you're starting in spring, bear in mind that the summer sun will be higher and might bypass some obstacles, providing more light than you'd expect.

Water: A Vital Resource

Water is another fundamental component of plant life. It's not just the medium through which nutrients are transported within the plant, but also a critical element for photosynthesis. Each plant species has its own water needs, with some requiring a steady supply of moisture and others preferring drier conditions.

Urban gardeners often have to rely on municipal water supplies to irrigate their plants. While this is usually safe, it's worth checking your local water quality report to ensure there are no harmful chemicals or heavy metals in the water that could affect your plants or your health.

You also need to understand your garden's water dynamics. Is your potential garden space prone to water logging, or does it dry out quickly? If you're gardening on a balcony or rooftop, does water pool after a rainstorm or does it drain away quickly?

These factors will influence not just what you can grow, but also how you design your garden to manage water efficiently. Techniques such as rainwater harvesting or installing a drip irrigation system can help make your urban garden more sustainable and water-efficient.

The Weather: Friend and Foe

Last but not least, understanding your local weather patterns and climate is essential. The temperature, humidity, wind speed, and precipitation levels all influence a plant's growth and health.

Urban environments often experience what is known as the 'urban heat island effect', where the city is noticeably warmer than the surrounding rural areas. This is due to factors such as heat-absorbing concrete and asphalt, the lack of vegetation, and waste heat produced by buildings and vehicles. This can make your city garden more susceptible to heat stress in the summer, requiring you to take measures to protect your plants.

Wind is another critical consideration, especially for rooftop or balcony gardens. High winds can damage plants, dry out the soil, and even knock over pots and planters. Some form of wind-break or shielding might be necessary to protect your plants in these exposed locations.

A city's weather patterns can also be quite unique, influenced by its geographical location, surrounding landscape, and the urban environment itself.

Familiarize yourself with the average temperatures throughout the year, when to expect the first and last frosts, average rainfall, and any common extreme weather events.

All this information can guide your decisions on what to plant and when, as well as how to protect your garden from the elements.

While weather conditions may seem a tad unpredictable and overwhelming, remember that there are many resources available to urban gardeners. Local extension services, gardening clubs, and online gardening communities can provide localized advice and support based on their own experiences with the same weather conditions.

A Practical Approach

Now that we've discussed the importance of sunlight, water, and weather, let's look at how you can practically assess these conditions in your potential urban garden space.

1. **Sunlight Mapping:** Spend a day observing how the sun moves across your space. Note down the times when the area is in full sun, partial sun, or full shade. Repeat this exercise in different seasons if possible. This exercise will give you a 'sunlight map' of your space, guiding your plant placement and selection.
2. **Water Assessment:** Check your water supply for any restrictions and its quality. Observe how rainwater behaves in your space. Does it pool or drain away quickly? This will help you understand

if you need to improve your space's drainage or if you can utilize techniques like rainwater harvesting.
3. **Weather Data:** Use online resources to find detailed climate data for your city. This should include average temperatures, frost dates, and rainfall levels. If you have a weather station nearby, this could provide more localized data.
4. **Wind:** Assess the windiness of your location, especially if it's an elevated site like a balcony or rooftop. You might need to plan for windbreaks or choose hardy plants that can withstand the wind.
5. **Microclimates:** Finally, remember that your garden could have microclimates - small areas where the climate differs from the surrounding area. A wall that receives a lot of sun could create a warmer microclimate, while a shady corner could be cooler and damper. These microclimates can be utilized to grow a wider variety of plants.

By thoroughly assessing the sunlight, water, and weather conditions in your urban garden, you can create an environment where plants not only survive but thrive. It's about working with nature, rather than against it, and using what you have to the best of your ability.

Adapting to Your Conditions
Once you've assessed your sunlight, water, and weather conditions, you can begin to plan your garden. This is where the real fun begins – selecting the right plants for your conditions.

Many plants are flexible and can adapt to a variety of conditions, but they will only truly thrive when their needs align with their environment. For instance, if your garden area is a sun-soaked rooftop, heat-tolerant plants like tomatoes, peppers, or Mediterranean herbs might do well. On the other hand, a shady balcony could be perfect for leafy greens or shade-tolerant herbs like mint or chives.

Adapting to your conditions also means learning to work with the weather, not against it. If you're in a region with a dry season, consider using drought-tolerant plants or employing water-saving techniques like mulching or drip irrigation.

If your area tends to be cool and damp, focus on plants that enjoy those conditions, like peas or kale, and use techniques to improve drainage in your garden beds.

The Art of Observation

In many ways, assessing sunlight, water, and weather conditions is all about developing your skills of observation. It's about slowing down, paying attention, and learning to read the subtle signs in your environment. It's also about becoming a part of your local gardening community.

Reach out to other gardeners in your area. They're an invaluable resource for understanding your local conditions and what works best in your region. Local extension services, community gardens, and horticultural societies are all excellent places to connect.

Remember, every garden is unique, and what works in one might not work in another. But that's part of the joy of gardening – it's a constant journey of discovery, experimentation, and, occasionally, serendipity.

In the end, the greatest gardens are not necessarily the ones with the most perfect conditions, but the ones where the gardener has learned to work in harmony with their unique slice of the environment.

It's a form of partnership – a symbiotic relationship between the gardener, the plants, and the local ecosystem. And it's a partnership that can yield not just abundant harvests, but also a deeper connection with the world around us.

As you step into the world of urban gardening, may you find that connection, and may your garden be a source of joy, wonder, and plentiful bounty.

Chapter 3: Selecting the Right Plants for Urban Gardening

Native Plants and Their Benefits

The urban gardener faces a unique set of challenges when it comes to selecting the right plants for their garden. The constraints of space, the often-limited availability of sunlight, and the unique microclimates created by city buildings and streets can make it tough to cultivate a thriving urban garden. One solution to these challenges lies in an approach that may seem counterintuitive in the concrete jungle: turning to native plants.

Native plants, as the name suggests, are plants that have evolved in a particular region over thousands, or even millions of years. These plants have adapted to local conditions and have developed a symbiotic relationship with the local fauna, soil microbes, and other plants. Because of this, native plants offer a host of benefits that can make them an ideal choice for the urban gardener.

To start with, native plants are hardy. They've spent countless generations adapting to the specific conditions of your region. They know how to survive the harshest summers, the coldest winters, and everything in between. This resilience makes them perfect for urban environments where unpredictable conditions are par for the course. Where a more delicate, non-native plant might struggle, native plants can thrive.

Additionally, native plants generally require less maintenance than their non-native counterparts. They've adapted to thrive in your local soil, so they usually don't need as much, if any, additional fertilization. They're used to your local rainfall patterns, so they often don't require extra watering. Less watering also means a more sustainable garden, as water conservation becomes increasingly important in our changing climate. Not to mention, less maintenance frees up more of your time to simply enjoy the fruits of your gardening labor.

Beyond hardiness and low maintenance, native plants also offer significant benefits for local wildlife. They provide food and shelter for local insect and bird populations. For example, native plants can support up to 3 times more species of native bees than non-native plants. This is particularly important in urban areas, where habitat loss can put pressure on local wildlife populations. By choosing native plants, you're not just creating a garden; you're creating a habitat.

Moreover, native plants contribute to the preservation of local biodiversity. Each plant species has a role to play in its ecosystem, from the smallest ground cover to the tallest tree.

By incorporating native plants into your garden, you're helping to preserve the complex web of life that makes up your local ecosystem. This, in turn, can contribute to a healthier and more resilient environment overall.

Now, while the benefits of native plants are many, it's important to remember that not all native plants will be suitable for every urban garden. Factors such as available space, light conditions, and soil type all come into play when selecting the right plants. Fortunately, there are resources available to help guide you in the right direction.

Local extension services, botanical gardens, and native plant societies often provide plant lists tailored to specific regions and conditions. These lists can be an invaluable tool for the urban gardener looking to incorporate native plants into their garden.

Native plants offer a sustainable, resilient, and biodiverse solution to the challenges of urban gardening. By choosing native plants, you're not just cultivating a garden; you're cultivating a piece of your local ecosystem. This approach to gardening can bring not only aesthetic and practical benefits but also a deep sense of connection to the natural world around you, even in the heart of the city.

The humble act of planting a seed can become an act of conservation, of resilience, of hope. So, as you plan your urban garden, consider going native. Your garden, your local wildlife, and your local ecosystem will thank you.

Easy-to-Grow Vegetables and Herbs

For the urban gardener looking to incorporate edibles into their green space, the selection of the right plants can make a world of difference.
Let's focus on those easy-to-grow vegetables and herbs that can provide fresh, nutritious produce, even in the most compact of city gardens.
From rooftop containers to balcony hanging baskets and from window boxes to small backyard plots, these plants can turn any urban space into a veritable cornucopia.

Firstly, let's talk about leafy greens. Spinach, lettuce, kale, and Swiss chard are all fantastic choices for the urban gardener. These plants are not only compact, making them perfect for container gardening, but they also grow quickly and continuously produce leaves throughout the season. Even better, many varieties are quite shade-tolerant, allowing you to make the most of those less sunny spots in your urban garden.

Another group of easy-to-grow plants are the root vegetables. Radishes, in particular, are a superstar in this category. With a fast growth rate (some varieties are ready to harvest in as little as three weeks) and a small footprint, radishes are perfect for urban gardens. Carrots and beets, while requiring a bit more patience, are also quite forgiving and can be grown in deep containers if ground space is limited.

Peas and beans are a boon to the space-challenged gardener. These plants grow vertically, meaning they take up minimal ground space. A trellis, a fence, even a balcony railing can serve as support for these prolific plants. Both peas and beans are relatively hardy, and as an added benefit, they enrich the soil with nitrogen, a nutrient essential to plant growth.

Tomatoes and peppers, while requiring a bit more sun, are also excellent choices for the urban garden. With many dwarf and bush varieties available, these plants can be grown in pots or hanging baskets. The joy of plucking a ripe tomato or pepper from your own plant is hard to beat.

Let's not forget about herbs. Herbs like basil, parsley, chives, mint, and rosemary are perfect for urban gardens. They are generally compact, can often tolerate a range of light conditions, and are incredibly useful to have on hand in the kitchen. An additional advantage of growing herbs is their aroma; they can turn your garden into a sensory delight.

All these plants share a few common characteristics that make them well suited to urban gardening. They are generally hardy, can often tolerate less-than-ideal light conditions, and are compact enough to be grown in containers. Plus, they are incredibly useful. From salads to soups and from stir-fries to sauces, these plants can transform your cooking.

A couple of tips can help increase your success with these easy-to-grow plants.

Firstly, good quality soil is key. Whether you're growing in the ground or in containers, ensure your plants have access to nutrient-rich, well-draining soil.

Secondly, regular watering is important, especially for container-grown plants.

Finally, don't forget about sunlight. While many of these plants can tolerate partial shade, all plants need some amount of sunlight to grow.

Remember, gardening is a learning process. Some plants will thrive, others might struggle. The important thing is to observe, learn, and most importantly, enjoy the process. With these easy-to-grow vegetables and herbs, even the smallest urban space can become a thriving, productive garden.

Best Plants for Small Spaces and Urban Environments

In the realm of urban gardening, creativity, and strategic plant selection are paramount. With limited space and varying environmental conditions, it's essential to choose plants that can adapt and thrive under these circumstances.

Here, we delve into some of the best plants for small spaces and urban environments that will transform your concrete vista into a verdant oasis.

Let's begin with a group of plants that thrive upwards rather than outwards: climbing and trailing plants. These are a boon for space-starved gardeners. Clematis, morning glory, and sweet peas are all excellent choices. These vigorous climbers will happily scale a trellis or fence, providing a stunning vertical display.

Likewise, trailing plants like ivy, creeping thyme, and certain varieties of nasturtiums can be used to add greenery to walls or to cascade from hanging baskets or window boxes.

Small trees and shrubs can also play a role in urban gardens. Dwarf fruit trees like apple, pear, and cherry can be grown in containers and can provide not only a lush, green canopy but also a bounty of fresh fruit.

Compact shrubs like boxwood, azalea, or hydrangea can add structure and year-round interest to your garden.
And let's not forget about ornamental grasses such as blue fescue or fountain grass. These plants add texture and movement and are typically quite drought tolerant, making them a low-maintenance option for urban gardens.

Next, consider plants that can endure the unique conditions of an urban environment. Many cities have what's known as a "heat island effect," where the city's concrete and buildings absorb and re-emit the sun's heat, causing temperatures to be higher than in surrounding rural areas. Plants like sedum, lavender, and ornamental sage are all heat-loving and can thrive in these conditions.

Urban environments are also often windy due to the tunnel effect created by buildings. Hardy grasses and perennials, such as switchgrass and echinacea, can tolerate wind and can add a touch of natural beauty to your urban garden. Similarly, ferns, hostas, and hellebores are all shade-loving plants that can prosper in the shadows of buildings.

For truly compact spaces, consider succulents and cacti. These plants come in an array of shapes, sizes, and colors, and they are masters of survival in harsh conditions. Many succulents and cacti are also quite slow-growing, meaning they won't outgrow their containers quickly.

Lastly, a small space needn't mean you forego a vegetable garden. As mentioned in the previous chapter, many vegetables and herbs can be successfully grown in pots. Cherry tomatoes, herbs, spinach, and peppers are all excellent choices for small-space gardening.

Remember that urban gardening is not just about overcoming challenges; it's also about embracing opportunities. The unique conditions of an urban environment can allow you to experiment with plants and planting styles that you might not consider in a more traditional garden setting.

From rooftop container gardens to vertical wall gardens, from window box herb gardens to balcony hanging baskets, urban gardening provides a wealth of opportunities to get creative and transform your small space into a thriving, green retreat.

So go forth, urban gardeners, and remember that with the right plants, even the smallest of spaces can become a sanctuary of greenery amidst the hustle and bustle of city life.

Ornamental vs. Edible: Balancing Aesthetics and Function

Urban gardening presents the unique opportunity to blend the ornamental and the edible, to intertwine aesthetics and function. Here, we explore how to strike a balance between these two elements, creating a garden that is not only pleasing to the eye but also bountiful in its yield.

One might think that ornamental and edible plants are fundamentally different. While it's true they each have their unique characteristics, the line between them is not as clear-cut as it may seem. Many plants, in fact, fit comfortably into both categories. They are the workhorses of the urban garden, providing both visual interest and food.

Edible plants like rainbow chard, red-veined sorrel, or purple kale can be stunning in their own right, their vibrant colors and textures rivaling those of many purely ornamental plants. Berries, too, add splashes of color and provide a delicious harvest. Redcurrants, blackberries, and strawberries are not only productive but also quite decorative.

Herbs are another group of plants that easily straddle the ornamental-edible divide. Lavender, rosemary, and thyme are all highly aromatic, visually pleasing, and culinarily useful. They can be used to create a sensory border, their scent wafting through your garden each time you brush past them.

Alternatively, ornamental plants can play a crucial role in an edible garden. They can provide structure, contrast, and seasonal interest. Tall ornamental grasses, for example, can serve as a backdrop for lower-growing edibles, while flowering plants can add color and attract beneficial insects.

The key to balancing aesthetics and function in an urban garden lies in thoughtful planning and design. Consider the overall look you want to achieve, as well as the practicalities of what you want to grow. Layering plants with different heights, colors, and textures can create a sense of depth and abundance even in a small space. Pairing plants with contrasting foliage can create visual interest, while grouping similar plants can create a sense of harmony and cohesion.

Edibles don't have to be relegated to a separate vegetable garden; they can be interspersed with ornamentals in borders, beds, and containers. This approach, known as edible landscaping or foodscaping, can create a garden that is both beautiful and bountiful.

At the same time, remember to account for the specific needs of each plant. While a particular arrangement might look good on paper, it's important to ensure that each plant is in a location where it can thrive. Consider factors like sunlight, soil type, and water requirements when deciding where to place each plant.

Lastly, don't forget about the seasons. A well-designed garden can provide year-round interest, with different plants taking center stage at different times of the year. Spring bulbs, summer berries, autumn leaves, and winter structure can all play a part in your garden's yearly cycle.

In essence, the balance between ornamental and edible in an urban garden is not so much a balance as a blend. The two can coexist, complement, and even enhance one another. With careful planning and a bit of creativity, you can create a garden that feeds both the body and the soul. It's a unique pleasure of urban gardening, a reminder that even in the heart of the city, we can cultivate beauty and bounty side by side.

Seasonal Considerations

An understanding of the seasons is a fundamental part of gardening. Seasonal considerations guide us not only in terms of what to plant and when, but they also influence our maintenance practices and help us to create a garden that provides year-round interest. In this chapter, we will explore some of the key seasonal considerations for the urban gardener.

The cycle of the gardening year typically begins in spring. This is the time for planting many types of seeds and seedlings, including cool-season vegetables like lettuce, peas, and spinach.

It's also the time to plant spring-flowering bulbs and to prune certain types of shrubs and trees. Spring is a time of rapid growth and renewal, and it provides the urban gardener with a chance to refresh and replant after the winter.

As we move into summer, the focus shifts towards maintenance and harvest. Watering becomes crucial, especially for container plants, which can dry out quickly in the summer heat.

This is also the time to harvest many types of vegetables and herbs, and to enjoy the vibrant colors of summer-flowering plants. Be vigilant about pests and diseases, which can become more prevalent in the warm, humid conditions of summer.

Fall is a time of transition in the garden. As the weather cools, it's time to harvest late-summer and fall crops like tomatoes, peppers, and winter squash. It's also the time to plant bulbs for spring flowering, and to start preparing the garden for winter. This can include tasks like adding compost or mulch to beds, bringing in or protecting tender plants, and cleaning and storing tools.

Winter, though often overlooked in the gardening calendar, is also an important season. For the plants, it's a time of rest and dormancy. For the gardener, it's a time for planning and preparation.

This is the time to order seeds, plan the layout for the coming year, and perform maintenance tasks like sharpening tools. It's also the time to enjoy the structural elements of the garden, like the bare branches of trees or the architectural form of evergreen shrubs.

In addition to these general considerations, it's important to keep in mind that each region will have its own unique seasonal patterns. Factors like frost dates, rainfall patterns, and temperature fluctuations will all influence what you can grow and when.

Furthermore, urban environments can have microclimates that differ significantly from the surrounding areas. Buildings can create wind tunnels or shade, while pavement and concrete can increase heat.

These factors can influence the local growing conditions and should be taken into account when planning and maintaining your garden.

An understanding of seasonal considerations is a key component of successful gardening. The rhythm of the seasons guides the cycle of planting, growth, harvest, and rest. As urban gardeners, tuning into this rhythm allows us to work with nature, rather than against it, and to create gardens that are not only productive, but also resilient and in harmony with the natural world.

By considering the seasons, we can make the most of each phase of the gardening year, creating a garden that brings joy and bounty all year round.

Chapter 4: Techniques for Maximizing Small Spaces

Vertical Gardening: Growing Upwards

There's a certain charm to the image of a sprawling garden, isn't there? Vast fields of marigold, rows upon rows of succulent tomatoes, and maybe even a little picturesque pond with lily pads afloat. But the reality of urban living can often be at odds with these bucolic dreams.

Fear not, because gardening is not a pursuit limited by space, but rather by imagination. Our cities are filled with untapped potential for green spaces: empty walls, tiny balconies, even the sides of buildings!

That's where the concept of vertical gardening comes in. It's all about growing upwards, maximizing limited space, and reaping bountiful harvests right in your own urban oasis.

Vertical gardening is not a modern fad. In fact, it has historical roots in ancient civilizations like the Hanging Gardens of Babylon. What we're doing is simply taking this age-old concept and adapting it to our contemporary needs. The principles are simple: start from the ground and work your way up.

To begin with, you'll need to select the right kind of plants for vertical growth. Some plants naturally lend themselves to this kind of cultivation.

Vining plants, such as tomatoes, cucumbers, and beans, are natural climbers and will readily ascend any structure you provide. But don't feel limited by these options.
With the right support, many plants can be encouraged to grow vertically, including some varieties of squash, melons, and even pumpkins.

Choosing the right support structure is the next step in your vertical gardening journey. Trellises, nets, and cages are common choices, each with its own set of advantages. A trellis, for example, can serve as a beautiful architectural element in your garden while providing robust support for your climbing plants.

On the other hand, nets can be easily installed and adjusted, and they offer flexibility in accommodating different plant sizes. Meanwhile, cages, particularly useful for heavier fruits like tomatoes, provide all-around support and can help maintain plant shape.

One of the beauties of vertical gardening is that it allows for creativity and customization. You could create a "living wall" with a series of hanging pots, for instance, or repurpose an old ladder into a unique plant stand. Even pallets can be transformed into vertical planters, and old shoe organizers can be filled with herbs to create a verdant, aromatic tapestry. The only limit is your imagination.

However, vertical gardening does require some particular considerations. For one, watering can be a challenge. Gravity can cause water to run down quickly, potentially leaving the upper plants dry and the lower ones waterlogged.

Consider installing a drip irrigation system to ensure even distribution of water. Similarly, nutrient distribution can also become an issue. Regular feeding with an appropriate fertilizer can help maintain the health of your vertical garden.

Light distribution is another key factor to consider. Remember, all plants need a certain amount of light to perform photosynthesis. In a vertical garden, upper-level plants may block the light from reaching those beneath them.

To avoid this, plan your garden carefully, placing taller plants on the top and smaller ones at the bottom. Also, consider the angle of sunlight throughout the day and across seasons.

Pest control and disease management may be easier in vertical gardens, as the improved air circulation helps prevent fungal diseases, and the height can deter some pests. However, regular inspection of your plants is always a good practice to catch any issues early.

In essence, vertical gardening is about turning constraints into opportunities. It's a testament to our human ingenuity and our innate connection with nature.

It invites us to look at our urban spaces differently, not as concrete jungles, but as vertical ecosystems brimming with potential.

It's a way to reclaim our connection with nature, to bring about a sense of peace and tranquility amidst the hustle and bustle of city life.

One of the most wonderful aspects of vertical gardening is its accessibility. You don't need a degree in horticulture to embark on this adventure. All you need is a little bit of space, a dash of creativity, and a whole lot of love for plants.

It doesn't matter if your available space is a small balcony, a sunny wall, or even just a windowsill, there's a vertical garden design waiting to spring to life.

In fact, many schools and community centers are catching on to the appeal of vertical gardening. It's a fantastic way to introduce children and young people to the joys of gardening.

There's something incredibly rewarding about planting a seed, watching it grow, and finally harvesting the fruits (or vegetables) of your labor. It teaches patience, responsibility, and an appreciation for the natural world.

Moreover, vertical gardening is an excellent way to enhance the aesthetics of your living space. Imagine stepping out onto your balcony and being greeted by a wall of vibrant marigolds, or preparing dinner with herbs plucked from your living wall in the kitchen.

It's about more than just the produce; it's about creating a space that's alive, that changes with the seasons, and that brings you joy every day.

And let's not forget the environmental benefits. Plants act as natural air purifiers, removing toxins from the air and releasing oxygen. They also help to reduce the urban heat island effect, a phenomenon where city areas are significantly warmer than their rural surroundings due to human activities. By growing a vertical garden, you're contributing to a healthier, more sustainable urban environment.

As you embark on your vertical gardening journey, remember that gardening is as much an art as it is a science. Don't be afraid to experiment with different plants and structures.

Keep a garden journal to track your progress and note any lessons learned along the way. Be patient, as good things take time. And most importantly, have fun with it. After all, gardening is not just about the destination - it's about the journey.

So, roll up your sleeves, put on your gardening gloves, and let's turn these urban spaces into lush, green, vertical gardens. The sky's the limit!

Container Gardening: Flexibility and Convenience

Let's now delve into another game-changer in the world of urban gardening - the art and science of container gardening. Picture this: a medley of pots brimming with leafy greens, vibrant flowers, and succulent fruits - all neatly arranged on your sunlit balcony or even indoors.
It's not just a pretty picture; it's a fully attainable reality. Container gardening is all about embracing flexibility and convenience, making it an ideal choice for the urban gardener.

The beauty of container gardening lies in its simplicity. All you need is a container, some quality potting soil, and a plant, and you're on your way. But the real magic happens when you start to explore the wealth of possibilities this form of gardening offers.

Let's start with the basics. Choosing the right container is crucial. While traditional pots and planters work wonderfully, don't limit yourself. Old buckets, wine crates, mason jars, even worn-out boots can serve as unique and charming plant homes. Just remember, any container you choose must have adequate drainage to prevent waterlogging.

The size of the container also matters. Small containers can dry out quickly, while very large ones can become waterlogged. As a general rule, match the size of the container to the size of the plant at maturity. This will help ensure that your plant has enough room to grow and thrive.

When it comes to filling your containers, regular garden soil won't do. It tends to be too heavy and may not drain well when used in a container. Instead, use a high-quality potting mix, which is lighter and designed to retain just the right amount of moisture.

Now comes the fun part: choosing your plants. One of the great joys of container gardening is the opportunity to experiment with a wide range of plants. From ornamental flowers to hearty vegetables, nearly anything can grow in a container with the right care. You can cultivate a mini herb garden in your kitchen, grow cherry tomatoes on your balcony, or even have a potted citrus tree in your living room.

The flexibility of container gardening also allows for better control over your plants' environment. Is it getting too hot for your shade-loving fern on the balcony? Simply move it to a cooler spot. Are your succulents not getting enough sun on your windowsill? Relocate them to a brighter location. This mobility is particularly beneficial when dealing with unpredictable urban weather or limited outdoor space.

Another notable advantage is the ease of pest and disease management. Isolated in containers, plants are less likely to fall victim to soil-borne diseases and pest infestations. If a problem does arise, it can be easier to address without the risk of it spreading to the rest of your garden.

But perhaps the most delightful aspect of container gardening is the creative expression it allows. You can play with different combinations of plants, colors, and textures to create stunning visual displays. You can arrange your containers in countless ways, change them with the seasons, or even design a whole container garden around a specific theme.

However, remember that container plants depend on you for their needs. Regular watering is crucial, as container plants can dry out quickly, especially in hot weather. They'll also rely on you for nutrients, as they can't draw from the earth as ground-planted counterparts do. Regular feeding with an appropriate fertilizer is a must.

So, whether you're a seasoned gardener looking to add variety to your green spaces, or a green-thumb-in-training starting your first gardening project, container gardening offers a world of possibilities. It's about growing without boundaries, about bringing life and color into our homes and urban spaces, one container at a time. Embrace the flexibility, enjoy the convenience, and most of all, have fun with it. You'll be amazed at the vibrant greenery you can cultivate in even the most compact of spaces.

Container gardening also provides an excellent opportunity for learning and experimentation. You can test different plant varieties, try out various potting mixes, or play with different watering schedules. It's a hands-on, interactive way to learn more about plant growth and care, which can be particularly engaging for children and beginners. Plus, the quick results and tangible progress can be incredibly satisfying and motivating.

Importantly, container gardening also extends the gardening season. Many plants that would otherwise be unable to survive the winter outdoors can be brought inside, allowing you to enjoy your green oasis all year round. This can not only brighten up your indoor spaces during the colder months, but also provide you with fresh herbs, vegetables, or fruits beyond their typical growing season.

Moreover, there's something profoundly rewarding about the sense of self-sufficiency that comes from growing your own food. It's about reconnecting with nature, understanding the cycles of growth, and appreciating the miracle of life, all from the comfort of your own home.

Additionally, container gardening can contribute to reducing your carbon footprint. Growing your own produce reduces the demand for commercially farmed goods and the associated transportation emissions. Plus, plants absorb carbon dioxide, helping to combat urban air pollution.

In the world of container gardening, there are no strict rules, only guidelines. Each container garden is a reflection of the individual who created it, making this form of gardening a truly personal and rewarding experience. From the choice of containers to the selection of plants, each decision offers an opportunity for self-expression.

So go ahead, let your imagination run wild. Convert that old teapot into a planter, or create a lush green corner in your living room. Mix and match your favorite herbs and flowers, or cultivate a rare plant variety. With container gardening, the world is your oyster - or should we say, your pot. It's time to embrace this flexible, convenient, and wonderfully rewarding form of urban gardening.

Hydroponics: Gardening without Soil

Let's now explore a gardening method that might initially sound like science fiction, but is increasingly becoming a go-to option for urban growers worldwide: hydroponics. This innovative approach to gardening takes us into a world where plants don't need soil to thrive. It's a fascinating exploration into how we can efficiently use our resources to cultivate plants, even in the most unlikely spaces.

Hydroponics, from the Greek words for 'water' and 'work', is a method of growing plants in a nutrient-rich, water-based solution. The plants are usually supported by an inert medium such as perlite, rock wool, clay pellets, or peat moss, which helps anchor the plant roots while giving them access to oxygen, an essential component of plant growth.

The beauty of hydroponic gardening lies in its efficiency and sustainability. Because the nutrients are delivered directly to the plant roots, plants grown hydroponically often grow faster and produce higher yields compared to their soil-grown counterparts. This method also uses less water, as the water in the system is recycled and reused, making hydroponics an eco-friendly choice for the conscientious urban gardener.

Starting a hydroponic garden may seem daunting, but don't let the technicalities deter you. The basic setup involves a growing tray, a reservoir filled with nutrient-enriched water, a submersible pump to move the water, and an air pump to oxygenate it. From this basic setup, you can venture into different hydroponic systems, such as Wick, Deep Water Culture (DWC), Nutrient Film Technique (NFT), or Aeroponics, each with its own advantages and ideal plant types.

One of the standout advantages of hydroponic gardening is its versatility. You can create a hydroponic system in various sizes to fit your available space. Whether you have a spacious basement or a small corner in your kitchen, you can set up a hydroponic garden. Plus, it's an excellent choice for urban dwellers who lack access to a garden or even a balcony, as it can be done entirely indoors.

When it comes to plant selection, hydroponics allows for a wide variety. Leafy greens like lettuce, spinach, and kale excel in hydroponic systems, as do herbs such as basil, dill, and parsley. Tomatoes, cucumbers, and peppers can also thrive, given enough light and the right setup. You can even grow strawberries hydroponically!

Lighting is a crucial factor in indoor hydroponic systems. While natural light is always best, most indoor setups require supplemental lighting. Fluorescent lights, compact fluorescent lights (CFLs), high-intensity discharge (HID) lights, and light-emitting diode (LED) lights are all suitable options. The choice depends on your budget, your plants' light requirements, and the size of your setup.

Hydroponics does require regular monitoring and maintenance. You'll need to keep an eye on the nutrient levels and pH of your water to ensure your plants are getting what they need. However, once you've gotten the hang of it, maintaining a hydroponic system can be less time-consuming than traditional gardening, as you won't have to deal with soil-related issues like weeds or pests.

This innovative method of gardening also serves as a fantastic educational tool. For children and adults alike, setting up and maintaining a hydroponic garden can be a great way to learn about plant biology and the importance of nutrients and pH levels. It's a hands-on, visual demonstration of how plants grow and thrive.

Hydroponic gardening is a testament to human ingenuity in the face of limited resources. It challenges the traditional notion of what a garden looks like and where it can exist. It's a method of growing that speaks to the heart of sustainable urban living, maximizing efficiency and output while minimizing waste.

The benefits of hydroponics extend beyond the practical. Just like traditional gardening, maintaining a hydroponic system can be a relaxing and rewarding pastime. Watching your plants grow and thrive in a system you've set up and maintained can bring a deep sense of satisfaction and connection to the natural world.

Furthermore, having a hydroponic system at home can provide you with fresh, pesticide-free produce year-round. No more worrying about the origin of your vegetables or the seasonality of your herbs. Your kitchen or living room can become a personal farmers market, offering you the freshest ingredients possible.

Hydroponic gardening also opens the door to unique aesthetic possibilities. Picture a living wall of leafy greens in your dining room, or a glowing cabinet of herbs in your kitchen. These systems can add an element of living art to your home, creating a space that's both visually appealing and functional.

Despite its high-tech image, you don't need a degree in botany or engineering to start a hydroponic garden. Many starter kits are available on the market, offering an easy entry point for beginners. These kits usually come with everything you need to start growing, including seeds, growing medium, nutrients, and a simple hydroponic system.

As you gain experience and confidence, you can begin to experiment with building your own systems, customizing them to fit your needs and your space. You can also delve into the world of aquaponics, a related method that combines raising fish with hydroponics in a mutually beneficial system.

Remember, like any other form of gardening, hydroponics is as much an art as it is a science. Each hydroponic garden is a unique ecosystem, reflecting the care, creativity, and passion of the gardener. So, don't be afraid to experiment, to learn, and to grow alongside your plants.

In conclusion, hydroponics offers a fascinating, efficient, and space-saving method for urban gardening. It's a testament to how far we've come in our understanding of plant growth and our ability to create sustainable food systems, even in the smallest and most unlikely of spaces. So why not give soil-less gardening a try? Who knows, you might just find that the future of gardening is floating right in your living room.

Window Gardening: Making Use of Natural Light

Next, let's explore a style of urban gardening that combines the simplicity of container gardening with the indoor comfort of hydroponics: window gardening. This method truly exemplifies the philosophy of "making the most of what you have." With a bit of creativity, even the narrowest window sill can be transformed into a miniature garden oasis.

Window gardening is all about harnessing the power of natural light to grow plants indoors. In an urban setting, windows often represent the most (and sometimes the only) direct access to sunlight within our homes. By placing plants in these lit areas, you can provide them with the energy they need to photosynthesize and grow, all without stepping foot outside.

The first step towards creating a window garden is assessing your available light. Not all windows are created equal, and the direction your window faces will determine the amount of sunlight it receives. South-facing windows generally receive the most light, followed by east and west-facing windows. North-facing windows receive the least light, but can still be suitable for certain low-light plants.

Once you've determined your light conditions, it's time to choose your plants. Most herbs, like basil, rosemary, and thyme, thrive in sunny windows.

Leafy greens, such as spinach, kale, and lettuce, can also do well. Succulents and cacti are excellent choices for bright, south-facing windows, while low-light plants like snake plants, pothos, and philodendrons can be perfect for less sunny spots.

Container choice is an essential aspect of window gardening. From traditional pots and planters to more creative options like mason jars, tin cans, or even repurposed wine bottles, there's a world of possibilities. The key is to ensure your container has adequate drainage and is the right size for your plant. Also, consider the weight of your container - especially if you're placing it on a narrow window sill.

One of the great advantages of window gardening is how it allows you to create microclimates within your home. Different windows may offer different light and temperature conditions, allowing you to grow a variety of plants that wouldn't normally thrive in the same space. This diversification can make for a visually stunning display and a wide array of fresh produce or herbs for your kitchen.

A critical factor in window gardening is regular monitoring of your plants. Indoor environments can often be dry due to heating or air conditioning, so regular watering is essential. However, be careful not to overwater, as this can lead to root rot and other issues. Also, keep an eye out for pests - while less common in indoor gardens, they can still occur.

Window gardening is not just about growing plants; it's about transforming your living space. A window filled with greenery can dramatically improve the ambiance of a room, making it feel more alive and connected to nature. It's about bringing the outside in, adding color and vibrancy to your urban home.

And let's not forget the mental and physical health benefits. Tending to your window garden can be a calming, meditative practice, offering a respite from the busy urban life. Plus, the plants can help purify the air in your home, contributing to a healthier living environment.

From a single pot of basil on a kitchen windowsill to a lush array of succulents on a sunny bay window, window gardening offers a world of opportunities. With a little creativity and care, you can harness the power of natural light to create your own indoor garden oasis, one window at a time.

So why wait? Let the light in and let your garden grow.

Chapter 5: Soil Management and Composting

The Importance of Healthy Soil

When it comes to the world of gardening, particularly in urban settings, soil often takes the limelight – and for good reason. This glorious, often underappreciated resource, is more than just dirt beneath our feet; it's a buzzing hub of life and the foundation of all thriving gardens.

If you're looking to grow healthy, vibrant plants in your urban space, understanding the importance of healthy soil is the first crucial step.

Soil is the lifeblood of our gardens, and its health directly influences the vitality of the plants it hosts. It's home to a rich tapestry of organisms, from bacteria, fungi, insects, to earthworms, which contribute to its fertility.
These tiny workers assist in breaking down organic matter, releasing essential nutrients back into the soil, and creating a porous structure ideal for root growth and water movement.

The health of soil is gauged by its fertility and structure. Fertile soil is packed with nutrients necessary for plant growth, while the structure relates to how well the soil holds together and its ability to retain water and air. In an urban environment, the challenge often lies in improving these two aspects of soil health. But worry not, because that's exactly what we'll be discussing in this chapter.

Creating Healthy Soil in Urban Spaces

Many novice urban gardeners may worry that city soil, tarnished by pollution and compaction, is beyond salvation. But with the right approach, any soil can be coaxed back to health. It all starts with observation and a little bit of soil science.

Take a handful of your garden soil, what do you see? Perhaps it's heavy and clumps together, or maybe it's sandy and loose. Each type of soil has its characteristics and presents different challenges and advantages. Clay soils, for example, are nutrient-rich but tend to waterlog, while sandy soils drain quickly but struggle to retain nutrients.

Soil amendments can improve these conditions. For heavy clay soils, incorporating organic matter like compost or well-rotted manure can improve its structure, making it lighter and more free-draining. On the other hand, sandy soils benefit from the addition of organic matter to enhance its nutrient-holding capacity and water retention.

Composting: The Urban Gardener's Secret Weapon

Composting is a wonderful solution for managing waste and improving soil health simultaneously. It's nature's way of recycling organic material, turning kitchen scraps, leaves, and garden waste into nutrient-rich compost that can be used to amend your soil.

Creating compost might seem like a daunting task for the urban gardener, but modern composting systems have made this practice more accessible than ever. You can choose from various options, such as traditional compost bins, worm composting (vermicomposting), or even bokashi composting, a Japanese method that effectively ferments organic waste.

Regularly adding compost to your garden soil improves its fertility and structure over time. Compost is rich in nutrients, providing a slow-release source of food for your plants.

It also improves the soil's ability to retain moisture, making your garden more resilient in times of drought. Moreover, it promotes the growth and activity of beneficial soil organisms, adding to the overall health of your garden ecosystem.

As urban gardeners, we have a unique opportunity to build a more sustainable relationship with our environment, even within the confines of concrete and steel. By understanding and nurturing our soil, and embracing practices like composting, we can transform our urban spaces into lush, productive gardens while reducing waste and promoting a healthier planet.

The soil under your feet, rich and complex, is more than a medium to grow plants; it's a world teeming with life, waiting to be discovered. So put on your gardening gloves, get a bit of dirt under your nails, and let's continue this journey of urban gardening.

Reaping the Benefits of Healthy Soil

With every handful of compost you mix into your soil, you are investing in the future of your urban garden. But the benefits of healthy soil extend beyond your garden's boundaries. Healthy soils are the unsung heroes of our environment, playing key roles in carbon sequestration, water purification, and supporting biodiversity.

Carbon sequestration is a fancy term for a simple process: the capture and storage of atmospheric carbon dioxide. Plants, through photosynthesis, absorb carbon dioxide, and as they grow and eventually die, this carbon is stored within the soil. By improving soil health, we can enhance this natural carbon sink, helping to mitigate climate change, right from our backyard!

Healthy soils also act as natural filters, purifying water as it percolates through the soil layers. This process helps maintain clean water sources and reduces the risk of harmful runoff entering our water systems. Plus, the improved water-holding capacity of healthy soils can mitigate the impacts of heavy rains, reducing the risk of flooding and erosion.

Soil is also a biodiversity hotspot. A single teaspoon of healthy soil can contain billions of microorganisms, including bacteria, fungi, and tiny invertebrates. These creatures form a complex food web that supports larger garden wildlife, such as birds and pollinators. By cultivating healthy soil, we are nurturing this biodiversity, contributing to a resilient and balanced ecosystem.

The Role of Soil Testing

As urban gardeners, we often inherit our soil, and it can come with its fair share of challenges, including potential contaminants. Soil testing is a valuable tool to understand the condition of your soil and guide your soil improvement efforts. It provides information on nutrient levels, pH, and in some cases, potential contaminants.

Testing your soil allows you to tailor your soil improvement strategies effectively. For instance, if your soil is deficient in a particular nutrient, you can choose specific amendments to address this. Similarly, knowing your soil's pH can guide your plant selection or inform the need to adjust the pH for certain crops.

Many local extension services offer soil testing, or you can purchase DIY soil testing kits for a quick assessment. Remember, soil health is not static; it changes over time with seasons and gardening practices. Regular soil testing can help you track these changes and adapt your garden practices accordingly.

Soil management and composting are pivotal practices for successful urban gardening. They are the keys to transforming our concrete jungles into lush, green, productive spaces.

By understanding and nurturing our soil, we can enjoy the bounty of fresh, homegrown food and contribute to a healthier, more sustainable urban environment.

Soil Testing and Amendments

Within the realm of gardening, the importance of understanding and improving your soil cannot be overstated. In this section, we're going to delve deeper into the practical aspects of soil health – soil testing and amendments.

Both of these elements serve as crucial tools in your gardening toolkit, allowing you to adapt your soil to suit the needs of your plants and improve its overall health.

The Why and How of Soil Testing

Soil testing is akin to a health check-up for your garden. It provides valuable information about the nutrient levels, pH balance, and in some cases, the presence of potential contaminants in your soil.

Why should we test our soil? Well, different plants have different nutrient needs and pH preferences. By knowing what's going on beneath the surface, you can tailor your gardening practices to suit your plants' needs. Are your tomatoes craving more calcium? Is your soil too alkaline for your blueberries? A soil test can help answer these questions.

Soil tests can be done through local extension services, or by using home testing kits available in garden stores or online. These tests usually involve collecting samples from different parts of your garden, mixing them together, and then sending off a small portion of this mix for analysis.

Remember, soil health is a dynamic state, changing with the seasons, the weather, and your gardening practices. It's good practice to test your soil every couple of years, or when you notice changes in plant health that you can't attribute to pests, diseases, or environmental conditions.

The Art of Soil Amendments

Once you have your soil test results, it's time to roll up your sleeves and dive into the world of soil amendments. Soil amendments are materials that you add to your soil to improve its physical properties, nutrient content, or pH level.

Organic matter, in the form of compost, well-rotted manure, or leaf mould, is the gardener's best friend when it comes to soil amendments.

Regular additions of organic matter can improve soil structure, boost nutrient levels, and increase the soil's capacity to hold water and air. It's a universal amendment that benefits all soil types, from heavy clays to light sandy soils.

For more specific soil issues, targeted amendments come into play. Lime or wood ash can be used to raise soil pH, making it more alkaline, while sulfur or peat moss can lower pH, increasing acidity.
If your soil test indicates a deficiency in a particular nutrient, specific amendments such as bone meal for phosphorus, or greensand for potassium, can be used.

Amending your soil is a process, not a one-time event. It takes time for these amendments to break down and their benefits to become available to your plants.

But with patience and regular care, you'll see the fruits of your labor in the form of healthier, more productive plants.

In a nutshell, soil testing and amendments are essential steps in successful urban gardening. They give you the power to understand and improve your soil, paving the way for a bountiful and sustainable urban garden.

So, get curious, be patient, and remember, every handful of soil you improve is a step towards a greener, more vibrant urban environment.

Understanding Soil Types and pH

Just as a chef needs to understand their ingredients to create a culinary masterpiece, a gardener must understand their soil to cultivate a thriving garden. Two fundamental aspects of soil that every gardener should get familiar with are soil type and pH. These factors significantly influence how your garden grows and how you can best manage it.

Soil Types: The Basics

Soils come in various types, each with its unique characteristics. The three primary types are sand, silt, and clay, and they're differentiated by the size of their particles. Most soils are a mix of these three types, and the proportion of each determines your soil's texture, drainage, and nutrient-holding capacity.

Sandy soils have large, coarse particles and feel gritty to the touch. They drain quickly, which can be a boon in rainy climates, but a challenge in dry ones, as they can struggle to retain water and nutrients.

Silt soils have medium-sized particles and a smooth, floury texture. They hold water better than sandy soils and are more fertile, but they can compact easily, which can hinder root growth.

Clay soils, with their tiny, tightly packed particles, feel sticky when wet and hard when dry. They're rich in nutrients and hold water well, but their poor drainage can lead to waterlogging.

Most gardeners dream of loam, a balanced mix of sand, silt, and clay, which combines the best characteristics of each soil type. It's fertile, well-draining, and easy to work with. But if you don't have loamy soil, don't despair! Understanding your soil type allows you to take steps to improve it, or to choose plants that thrive in your particular soil.

The Role of pH in Soil Health

Soil pH measures how acidic or alkaline your soil is. It's a crucial factor because it influences the availability of nutrients in your soil. Some nutrients become less available at high pH (alkaline conditions), while others become less available at low pH (acidic conditions).

The pH scale ranges from 0 to 14. A pH of 7 is considered neutral, while values below 7 indicate acidity, and values above 7 indicate alkalinity. Most plants prefer a slightly acidic to neutral pH, between 6 and 7, but some plants, like blueberries and rhododendrons, prefer more acidic soils.

Soil pH can be influenced by various factors, including the parent rock material, rainfall, and human activities. You can adjust your soil pH, within limits, using amendments. To increase pH, gardeners typically use lime, while sulfur is used to decrease pH. However, these adjustments are temporary and need to be repeated over time.

Understanding your soil type and pH is like having a roadmap to guide your gardening journey. It allows you to tailor your soil management practices and plant selection to your specific conditions, increasing your chances of gardening success. And remember, every soil type and pH has its advantages and challenges.

The key is to understand and work with what you have, making adjustments as needed, and always nurturing your soil's health. After all, healthy soil is the foundation of a thriving garden, and understanding it is the first step to becoming a successful urban gardener.

The Importance of Composting

As urban gardeners, we have a unique opportunity to transform our kitchen scraps and garden waste into black gold – compost. Composting is a natural process where organic materials break down into a rich, soil-like substance that works wonders for your garden. Let's delve into why composting is so important and how it can help us grow healthier, more productive plants in our urban spaces.

A Nutrient Powerhouse for Your Plants

Compost is rich in nutrients that plants need to grow and thrive. As the organic material breaks down, it releases nutrients like nitrogen, phosphorus, and potassium, also known as the 'big three' in the gardening world. But that's not all; compost also contains a host of micronutrients, such as calcium, magnesium, and iron, which are equally important for plant health.

The beauty of compost is that it releases these nutrients slowly, over time, providing a steady source of nourishment for your plants. This slow-release nature means there's less risk of nutrient runoff, a common problem with synthetic fertilizers, which can harm local waterways.

Improving Soil Structure and Fertility

Whether your urban garden boasts sandy soil, clay soil, or anything in between, compost can improve its structure. For sandy soils, compost helps increase water and nutrient retention. In clay soils, it improves drainage and reduces compaction, making it easier for plant roots to spread.

Adding compost also increases the amount of organic matter in your soil, which is key to soil fertility. Organic matter feeds soil organisms, from earthworms to microscopic bacteria, that contribute to the soil's health and fertility. These tiny creatures help further break down organic materials, cycling nutrients back into the soil and creating a rich, crumbly structure ideal for plant growth.

A Sustainable Way to Reduce Waste

In an urban environment, composting offers a practical and sustainable solution for managing organic waste. By composting our kitchen scraps, coffee grounds, and yard waste, we can significantly reduce the amount of waste that ends up in landfills, where it produces methane, a potent greenhouse gas.

Moreover, composting helps close the loop in our food system, turning waste back into a valuable resource. It's a tangible way we can contribute to sustainability right from our backyards or balconies.

Creating a Balanced Ecosystem

Healthy soil is the foundation of a balanced garden ecosystem. By adding compost to our gardens, we're not just feeding our plants; we're nurturing a whole community of soil organisms. These organisms contribute to pest and disease suppression, nutrient cycling, and improved soil structure, creating a resilient, self-regulating ecosystem.

Composting is more than just a gardening practice; it's a commitment to sustainability and a healthier urban environment. It's a testament to nature's ability to recycle and regenerate, turning waste into a resource that nourishes our gardens and feeds our cities. So, next time you toss those apple peels or coffee grounds into your compost bin, remember, you're not just making compost; you're making a difference.

Natural Fertilizers

As we continue our journey into urban gardening, let's explore another essential topic: natural fertilizers. These are the unsung heroes of the garden, providing essential nutrients to our plants in a sustainable, eco-friendly way. Unlike synthetic fertilizers, which can harm the environment and disrupt soil life, natural fertilizers nourish the soil, the plants, and the myriad of organisms that call your garden home.

The Scoop on Natural Fertilizers

Natural fertilizers, also known as organic fertilizers, come from plant, animal, or mineral sources. They're typically slower to break down than synthetic fertilizers, providing a steady supply of nutrients over a longer period. This slow-release nature makes them less likely to burn plants or leach into groundwater, a win for both your garden and the environment.

There's a wide range of natural fertilizers available, each with its unique nutrient profile. Let's take a look at some of the most commonly used ones.

Compost: As we've discussed, compost is an excellent soil amendment and a rich source of nutrients. Regular additions of compost can provide most, if not all, of the nutrients your plants need.

Manure: Well-rotted manure from herbivores, like cows, horses, or chickens, is another great natural fertilizer. It's rich in nitrogen, which promotes leafy growth, making it perfect for greens and lawns. Remember, always use well-rotted manure in your garden; fresh manure can burn plants and may contain pathogens.

Bone meal and blood meal: These are by-products of the meat processing industry. Bone meal is high in phosphorus, which is important for root development and flowering, while blood meal is a potent source of nitrogen.

Seaweed and fish emulsion: If you live near the coast, these are fantastic options. Seaweed can be used fresh or in a dried and powdered form, while fish emulsion is usually sold as a liquid. Both are rich in nutrients and trace elements.

Green manure: This involves growing a cover crop, like clover or vetch, and then digging it into the soil to decompose. The decomposing plants add nutrients to the soil and improve its structure.

Using Natural Fertilizers

When using natural fertilizers, the key is to match the fertilizer to your plants' needs. For example, a flowering plant preparing to set blooms will appreciate a boost of phosphorus from bone meal, while your leafy greens will thrive with the nitrogen provided by a well-rotted manure or blood meal.

Remember, balance is crucial. Over-fertilizing, even with natural fertilizers, can lead to excessive growth, making plants more susceptible to pests and diseases. It's always a good idea to test your soil before applying fertilizers to understand what nutrients your soil already has in abundance and what it may be lacking.

Natural fertilizers are a fantastic tool in the urban gardener's toolkit, allowing us to nourish our plants while caring for the environment. By understanding and using these fertilizers, we can create productive and sustainable urban gardens that are not just green spaces, but green in every sense of the word.

So, let's embrace these natural allies, and together, we can grow gardens that are as nourishing for the planet as they are for us.

Chapter 6: Natural Pest Control and Plant Care

Common Pests in Urban Gardens and How to Control Them

In the heart of the city, amid the hustle and bustle, the urban garden is a tranquil oasis. Concrete jungles give way to lush foliage, vibrant colors, and the rich, earthy scent of fertile soil. Yet, as any seasoned gardener will tell you, this serene sanctuary is not without its challenges. One such trial is the presence of unwelcome guests: pests.

Pests are an inevitable part of gardening, and urban spaces are no exception. Despite the concrete barriers, these tiny invaders find their way to your green haven, threatening your carefully cultivated plants.

But fear not!

With the right knowledge and a little patience, you can keep these nuisances at bay using natural, sustainable methods. Let's explore some of the most common urban garden pests and how to control them.

Aphids: The Tiny Terrors

Aphids are minute, sap-sucking insects that come in various colors. They're common in urban gardens, particularly on new growth or undersides of leaves. They reproduce rapidly, and a small aphid population can soon overrun your garden.

To control aphids, consider introducing beneficial insects, such as ladybugs and lacewings, which are natural aphid predators. You can also make a simple homemade spray by mixing a few drops of mild dish soap with water. Spraying this on infested plants will cause the aphids to dehydrate and die. Always remember to rinse your plants with clear water a few hours after application to prevent any soap damage.

Slugs and Snails: The Silent Munchers

Slugs and snails are notorious for their love of leafy greens and tender plants. These nocturnal creatures can cause significant damage overnight, leaving you with chewed leaves and a heavy heart.

One effective way to deter these pests is by creating barriers. Coffee grounds, crushed eggshells, or diatomaceous earth around your plants can deter them, as these materials are abrasive to the soft bodies of slugs and snails. Additionally, consider setting up a beer trap. The yeast in beer attracts them, and they'll fall into the trap and drown.

Spider Mites: The Webspinners

Spider mites are tiny creatures that are often overlooked until it's too late. They thrive in hot, dry conditions, spinning fine webs on plant leaves and stems. Mites suck plant juices, causing leaves to yellow and drop off.

A simple way to manage a spider mite infestation is by regularly spraying your plants with water. This not only hydrates your plants but also disrupts the mites' lifecycle. Introducing predatory insects like ladybugs and predatory mites can also help keep their population in check.

Cabbage Worms: The Leaf Decimators

If you're growing brassicas—cabbage, kale, broccoli, and the like—you'll likely encounter cabbage worms. These green caterpillars blend well with the leaves they feed on, making them hard to spot until they've caused significant damage.

Handpicking is an effective, albeit time-consuming, method of controlling cabbage worms. For a more hands-off approach, consider using a natural bacterial insecticide known as Bacillus thuringiensis (Bt). When the caterpillars ingest this bacterium, they stop eating and die within days.

Ants: The Underground Invaders

While ants can help with decomposition and turning soil, a large infestation can be problematic, especially if they're farming aphids for honeydew (a sweet secretion).

Cinnamon is a natural ant deterrent; sprinkling it around your plants can help keep ants at bay. You can also make a borax bait. The ants are attracted to the sugar in the bait, but the borax is toxic to them. They'll carry the bait back to their colony, effectively controlling the population. However, please use this method with caution, especially if you have pets or children, as borax can be harmful if ingested.

Fungus Gnats: The Root Destroyers

Fungus gnats are small, dark, fly-like pests that primarily pose a threat to young plants and seedlings. The adult gnats are merely annoying, but the larvae feed on plant roots, which can stunt growth and even kill your plants.

One of the easiest ways to prevent fungus gnat infestations is by not overwatering your plants. Fungus gnats thrive in damp environments, so allowing the soil to dry out between waterings can help keep their population in check. Yellow sticky traps can also be effective in catching adult gnats.

Whiteflies: The Ghostly Fliers

Whiteflies are tiny, white, moth-like insects that suck plant sap and excrete honeydew, much like aphids. This can lead to sooty mold and can weaken your plants over time.

Control whiteflies by introducing beneficial insects like ladybugs, lacewings, and predatory wasps. Reflective mulches can also deter whiteflies. If you need a stronger approach, consider insecticidal soaps or oils.

Rodents: The Furry Foes

In urban environments, it's not uncommon to have rodents visit your garden. Rats and mice can damage your plants by eating fruits, vegetables, and plant parts.

To deter rodents, keep your garden clean and free from food scraps. Install a mesh fence around your garden to keep them out. If the problem persists, consider humane traps.

Remember, the goal of pest management isn't to eradicate these creatures completely, but to maintain a balanced ecosystem. Integrated Pest Management (IPM) is a holistic, sustainable approach to pest control that involves multiple strategies such as biological control, use of resistant plant varieties, and modification of gardening practices.

It focuses on long-term prevention of pests or their damage through a combination of techniques such as fostering beneficial insects and using natural pesticides.

While pests can be a nuisance, they also offer an opportunity to understand and interact with nature more intimately. As an urban gardener, you are not just a cultivator of plants but a steward of the tiny patch of earth under your care. You have the power to create an environment that supports life, promotes biodiversity, and contributes to the overall health of our planet.

Plant Care: Watering, Pruning, and Fertilizing

Caring for your urban garden is as much an art as it is a science. It's a harmonious blend of understanding your plants' needs and responding with the right care techniques.

Among the many aspects of plant care, three stand out as vital: watering, pruning, and fertilizing. Let's delve into these practices and how they can help your urban garden flourish.

Watering: The Lifeblood of Your Garden

Water is essential for all life, and your plants are no exception. However, each plant has unique watering requirements that depend on its species, size, and stage of growth, as well as the season and the local climate. Overwatering can be as harmful as underwatering, leading to root rot and other fungal diseases.

One common rule of thumb is to water deeply but infrequently, encouraging your plants to develop deep, robust root systems. Use your finger to check soil moisture: if the top inch or so is dry, it's likely time to water. Water in the early morning or late evening to reduce evaporation, and aim at the base of your plants to avoid soaking the foliage, which can lead to diseases.

Keep in mind that container plants often require more frequent watering, as pots can dry out quicker than garden beds. Also, certain plants, like succulents, prefer their soil to dry out completely between watering, so adjust your watering schedule based on your garden's specific needs.

Pruning: The Art of Selective Trimming

Pruning involves selectively removing certain parts of a plant, such as branches, buds, or roots, to improve the plant's health, control growth, or enhance flowering or fruiting. It's like giving your plants a haircut, except that it can profoundly affect their growth and productivity.

Regular pruning can help increase light and air penetration, reducing the likelihood of disease and pest infestations. It can also direct a plant's energy towards producing more flowers or fruits, instead of unwanted or excessive leafy growth.

Always use clean, sharp tools when pruning to avoid causing unnecessary stress or injury to your plants. Prune just above a bud or side branch, and don't remove more than a third of a plant's growth at a time. The best time to prune depends on the plant, but generally, it's best to prune during the plant's dormant season.

Fertilizing: Feeding Your Green Friends

Just like humans, plants need a balanced diet to thrive. They draw nutrients from the soil, and over time, these nutrient reserves can become depleted, especially in an urban garden where space is limited. That's where fertilizers come in.

Fertilizers can be organic or synthetic, but for the sake of sustainability, let's focus on organic fertilizers, such as compost, manure, bone meal, or fish emulsion. These not only provide essential nutrients but also improve soil structure, promote beneficial soil microbes, and are less likely to cause nutrient burn compared to synthetic fertilizers.

When fertilizing, remember the adage "less is more." Overfertilization can lead to excessive, weak growth and even damage your plants. Also, different plants have different nutrient needs, so tailor your fertilizing practices to each plant's requirements.

The key to successful urban gardening lies in understanding your plants and providing them with the care they need. Gardening is not a one-size-fits-all endeavor; it's a deeply personal journey that evolves over time.

So, embrace the learning process, and remember, every green thumb has first had to weather a few brown leaves.

Planting and Care for Edible Gardens

The joy of plucking a ripe tomato from your garden or snipping fresh herbs for your dinner is unparalleled. Growing your own food is not only rewarding but also a powerful step towards sustainability. Here, we delve into the world of edible gardening in the urban landscape, covering everything from planting to nurturing your homegrown produce.

Choosing the Right Plants

The first step in setting up your edible garden is choosing what to grow. This decision is influenced by your taste preferences, the space you have available, and your local climate.

For beginners, it's often best to start with easy-to-grow vegetables and herbs like lettuce, radishes, basil, or chives.

These plants are typically hardy, grow fast, and don't require much space or care.

If you have a bit more room or are up for a challenge, you can branch out into growing plants like tomatoes, peppers, cucumbers, or even small fruit trees.

Planting Basics

Once you've chosen your plants, the next step is planting them. There are two main ways to start your edible garden: from seeds or from young plants, often called "transplants" or "seedlings."

Starting from seeds is often cheaper and offers a wider variety of options. However, it requires more time and care. If you choose this route, follow the planting instructions on the seed packet. Some seeds need to be started indoors before being transplanted outside.

Transplants, on the other hand, give you a head start. They're especially useful for slow-growing or heat-loving plants like tomatoes and peppers.

Whether you're planting seeds or transplants, make sure to give your plants enough space to grow. This includes room for their roots in the soil and space above ground for branches and leaves.

Watering and Feeding Your Edible Garden

As we discussed earlier, correct watering is crucial. Most edible plants prefer consistently moist, but not waterlogged, soil. Mulching around your plants can help conserve moisture and reduce the frequency of watering.

Fertilizing is equally important in an edible garden, as you want your plants to produce as much as they can. Compost or well-rotted manure are excellent organic choices, providing a slow-release source of nutrients. It's also beneficial to add specific fertilizers based on your plants' needs, like bone meal for root crops, or potassium-rich fertilizers for fruiting plants.

Pest Control and Maintenance

In an edible garden, pest control must be handled carefully, as you'll be eating these plants. The methods described earlier, such as introducing beneficial insects, using homemade sprays, and maintaining plant health, are especially relevant here.

Regular maintenance is also key. This includes weeding, removing dead or diseased plant material, and monitoring for pests and diseases. A well-maintained garden is not only more productive but also more resilient.

Harvesting

The last step, and certainly the most rewarding, is harvesting. Each plant has its own cues for when it's time to harvest: tomatoes change color, beans and peas fill out their pods, leafy greens reach a certain size. Regular harvesting often encourages more production.

An edible garden is a living, thriving entity, and each plant contributes its own character. It's an ongoing journey of learning, observing, and adapting. As an urban gardener, you're not just growing food; you're nurturing a slice of nature in the heart of the city, and that's something truly special.

Planting and Care for Ornamental Gardens

The beauty and tranquillity of an ornamental garden is an oasis in the urban jungle. These gardens, cultivated for their aesthetic appeal rather than edible produce, are a canvas for your creativity. They offer an array of colors, textures, and scents, and can attract a variety of birds and insects, enhancing local biodiversity. Here, we delve into the art and science of creating and caring for your urban ornamental garden.

Choosing the Right Plants

The plant selection process for an ornamental garden is a delightful exploration of the senses. From fragrant roses to stunning hydrangeas, trailing ivy to statuesque ferns, the options are nearly limitless.

When selecting plants, consider their growth habits, mature size, color, and seasonal changes. Also, consider the conditions of your garden — the amount of sunlight it receives, the soil type, and your local climate. These factors will influence the types of plants that will thrive in your garden.

Planting Basics

As with edible gardens, ornamental plants can be started from seeds or transplants. Seeds offer more variety and the joy of watching a plant grow from the very beginning. Transplants, however, provide an instant visual impact and are often easier for beginners.

When planting, give each plant enough space to reach its mature size. This will ensure your garden doesn't become overcrowded and will allow each plant to showcase its beauty.

Watering and Feeding Your Ornamental Garden

Watering needs will depend on the type of plants in your ornamental garden. Succulents and drought-tolerant plants require less water, while ferns and certain flowering plants prefer consistently moist soil. As a general rule, it's better to water deeply and less frequently, promoting healthier root growth.

Fertilizing is also important for vibrant, healthy plants. Organic matter like compost or well-rotted manure can provide a wealth of nutrients and also improve soil structure. Some plants may require specific fertilizers, especially flowering plants, which can benefit from phosphorus-rich fertilizers.

Pest Control and Maintenance

Ornamental gardens can attract a variety of pests. However, a balanced garden ecosystem will often keep pest populations in check. Encourage beneficial insects and birds, which are natural predators of many pests. As with edible gardens, avoid harsh chemical pesticides, opting for natural alternatives whenever possible.

Regular maintenance, including pruning and deadheading, can keep your ornamental garden looking its best. Pruning helps maintain a plant's shape and size, while deadheading (removing spent flowers) encourages many species to produce more blooms.

Design and Aesthetic

Design plays a crucial role in ornamental gardening. Consider height, color, and blooming season when arranging your plants. Taller plants can act as a backdrop for shorter ones, while a mix of bloom times ensures you'll have color in your garden throughout the growing season.

Don't forget hardscape elements, like benches, trellises, or bird baths. These can add structure and interest to your garden, making it a welcoming space for both wildlife and people.

Creating an ornamental garden in an urban setting is a fulfilling endeavor. It's an opportunity to carve out a pocket of natural beauty within the city limits, a place where you can express your creativity and connect with the natural world. It's your personal sanctuary, a testament to the transformative power of plants.

Seasonal Care for Your Urban Garden

Just as the city changes with the seasons, so too does your urban garden. Each season brings its own delights and challenges, and understanding these can help you keep your garden healthy and vibrant throughout the year. Let's embark on a seasonal journey through the urban garden, exploring the unique care requirements of each period.

Spring: A Time for New Beginnings

Spring is a time of rebirth in the garden. As the weather warms, dormant plants awaken, and new growth appears. It's the perfect time to clean up any winter debris, prune any winter-damaged branches, and prepare your garden beds for planting.

Spring is also an excellent time to start many seeds, either indoors or directly in the garden, depending on the plant and your local climate. Keep a close eye on young plants, as they can be vulnerable to pests and diseases.

Summer: The Season of Growth and Harvest

Summer is a time of rapid growth and, in the case of edible gardens, plentiful harvests. Regular watering is crucial during this period, especially for container gardens, which can dry out quickly in the summer heat. However, be mindful of water restrictions in your urban area during the dry season.

Summer is also the prime time for pests and diseases, so maintain a regular schedule of monitoring and preventative care.

If you have a flowering garden, deadhead regularly to encourage continuous blooming. For your vegetable garden, frequent harvesting will often stimulate plants to produce more.

Autumn: The Time to Prepare and Plant

In the autumn, the pace of the garden slows down. As the weather cools, many plants start preparing for the winter ahead. This is the perfect time to plant perennials, including bulbs for spring bloom, as the cooler temperature and increased rainfall help establish roots.

Autumn is also the time for preparing your garden for the coming winter. Clean up fallen leaves and other plant debris to prevent disease, and consider mulching your beds to protect them from winter weather. If you have any tender plants, consider bringing them indoors or providing them with some form of frost protection.

Winter: The Season of Rest

Winter is a quiet time in the garden, but there's still work to be done. In regions with harsh winters, ensuring that your plants are well-protected from the cold is paramount. This can involve covering your plants with horticultural fleece or moving containers to a more sheltered location.

Winter is also the time to plan for the year ahead. While the garden lies dormant, take the time to reflect on the past growing season and to plan your garden for the next year. This can involve ordering seeds, planning new beds, or even just dreaming about the possibilities.

Each season in the urban garden is a celebration of life's cycles, a testament to the resilience of nature even in the heart of the city. By understanding and working with these seasonal rhythms, you can create a garden that is not only beautiful and productive but also in harmony with the natural world.

Chapter 7: Setting up and Maintaining Different Types of Urban Gardens

Designing an Edible Garden

Welcome, dear reader, to what I personally consider to be one of the most exciting chapters in our urban gardening journey. We are now going to delve into the practical, hands-on aspect of urban gardening: designing your very own edible garden.

In an urban environment, it can sometimes feel like the odds are stacked against you when it comes to growing your own food. The challenges of limited space, lack of sunlight, and city pollution can seem insurmountable, but fear not! By the end of this chapter, you will have all the knowledge you need to transform even the smallest city balcony or dingiest courtyard into a verdant oasis, brimming with delicious, home-grown produce.

First, let's talk about space. Space is, of course, the most glaring challenge for the urban gardener. But it's not about how much space you have, it's about how you use it. Vertical gardening, for instance, is an innovative method that makes the most of every square inch available. In a vertical garden, plants grow upwards on trellises, wall-mounted containers, or specially designed "green walls." It's a solution that's as aesthetically pleasing as it is practical, adding a lush, green touch to your urban environment while providing a bounty of fresh produce.

Next, let's tackle sunlight. Most vegetables need at least six hours of sunlight each day to thrive. This can be a challenge in built-up areas where buildings block the sun for much of the day. But remember, there is a whole host of shade-tolerant veggies that can do well in less than ideal conditions. Leafy greens like spinach, lettuce, and kale, as well as root vegetables like carrots and beets, can often grow in partial shade. Moreover, reflective surfaces can be utilized to maximize the available light. Placing light-colored materials like white gravel or reflective film around your plants can help direct more sunlight onto your plants.

The key to a successful urban edible garden is to start with a solid plan. Begin by assessing your space. Measure out the area available, and take note of how much sun it gets throughout the day. Think about access to water, and consider where you might store tools and compost. This initial assessment is essential to decide what type of garden will work best in your space.

Once you have a good understanding of your space, start thinking about what you want to grow. While it's tempting to jump straight into exotic fruits and vegetables, it's usually best to start with easy-to-grow options that you know you will eat. Think tomatoes, cucumbers, bell peppers, herbs, and salad greens. These crops are ideal for beginners, and there's nothing like the satisfaction of eating a salad made entirely from your own urban garden.

Now that you've chosen what to grow, it's time to design your space. Use a piece of graph paper to draw a scale model of your garden area. Place taller plants like tomatoes and beans at the north end so they won't block sunlight from reaching smaller plants.

Remember, in a vertical garden, this might mean placing them lower down on the wall. Plan for the needs of each plant: some need more space, some need support to climb, and some prefer to be in pots rather than in the ground. This detailed planning stage can be incredibly satisfying. It's the moment when your dream garden starts to take shape.

The final step in designing your edible garden is to consider your soil. In urban areas, soil quality can vary significantly, and in many cases, the existing soil may not be suitable for growing vegetables. Raised beds filled with a mix of high-quality topsoil and compost can be an excellent solution, providing a nutrient-rich environment for your plants. Alternatively, you might choose to grow your plants in containers, where you have complete control over the soil and its nutrient content.

Soil isn't just about the dirt your plants are sitting in; it's a living, breathing ecosystem that's vital to the health of your garden. Good soil should be teeming with beneficial microbes that help your plants absorb nutrients. Regularly adding organic matter, like compost or worm castings, will ensure your soil stays healthy and nutrient-rich.

When it comes to containers, the world is your oyster. Traditional pots, window boxes, and hanging baskets are all fair game. But don't be afraid to get creative. Old boots, pallets, and even discarded kitchen sinks can become plant homes with a little imagination. The key is to ensure that any container you use has adequate drainage to prevent water logging.

Now that you've designed your garden, it's time to plant. Depending on what you're growing, you might start from seed or buy young plants, known as 'starts' or 'seedlings', from a garden center. Make sure to follow the instructions on the seed packet or plant label, especially when it comes to planting depth and spacing. Overcrowding plants can lead to poor air circulation and increase the likelihood of diseases.

Once your plants are in the ground, or pot, as the case may be, it's all about maintenance. Regular watering is crucial, especially for container plants which can dry out quickly. However, overwatering can be just as harmful, leading to root rot and other problems. As a general rule, water when the top inch of soil feels dry to the touch.

Fertilizing is another key aspect of garden maintenance. Even the best soil can become depleted of nutrients over time, especially if you're growing hungry crops like tomatoes or zucchini. Organic fertilizers, like seaweed emulsion or compost tea, can be applied regularly to keep your plants healthy and productive.

Pest control is a part of urban gardening, too. You might be surprised by how many critters can find their way into even the most concrete of jungles! The key to managing pests is to catch problems early. Regularly inspect your plants for signs of damage, and if you spot any pests, identify them before deciding on a course of action. Many pests can be managed with simple methods, like hand-picking or using a spray of water to knock them off the plant. Encouraging natural predators, like ladybugs and birds, can also be a great, environmentally friendly way to keep pests in check.

Your journey into edible gardening is a cycle, a beautiful, never-ending loop of learning, growing, harvesting, and planning for the next season. It's a hobby that requires dedication and patience, but the rewards are immense. There's nothing quite like the taste of a tomato you've grown yourself, or the satisfaction of seeing a plate full of food you've nurtured from seed to table.

Take it slow, allow yourself to make mistakes and learn from them. Remember, the goal is not perfection, but a deeper connection with the food you eat and the world you live in. So, roll up your sleeves, get your hands dirty, and let's start planting!

Designing Your Garden Layout

Taking a step further into our urban gardening adventure, we're now going to focus on the layout of your garden. This is the stage where your garden starts to feel real, a tangible vision rather than a dream. It's akin to sketching out the blueprint of a house, setting the foundation for all the beauty to come.

When designing your garden layout, remember that it's not just about aesthetics, although a visually pleasing garden is certainly a goal. Functionality and practicality should be your guiding principles, ensuring that your garden isn't just beautiful, but also productive and easy to manage.

Start by thinking about the path of the sun across your garden. Take note of which areas get the most sunlight, and at what times of day. This will influence the placement of your plants. Sun-loving veggies like tomatoes, peppers, and squash should be placed where they'll get at least six hours of sunlight each day. Shade-tolerant plants, like lettuce and spinach, can be placed in areas that get a bit less sun.

Next, consider access. You should be able to reach every plant in your garden without straining or stepping on other plants. This is especially important for tasks like weeding, pruning, and harvesting. In larger garden beds, consider creating access paths. Not only do these paths make maintenance easier, but they also add structure and visual appeal to your garden.

When deciding on the shape of your garden beds or pots, there's no one-size-fits-all answer. Rectangular or square beds are classic choices and can be a good fit for a more traditional garden layout. However, if your space is irregular or if you're looking for a more organic feel, don't be afraid to experiment with curved or free-form beds.

Plant placement is another critical factor to consider. A common mistake is to place plants too close together, which can lead to competition for nutrients, water, and light, and can also encourage the spread of diseases. On your garden layout, ensure each plant is allotted enough space based on its mature size, not its size at planting.

Taller plants should be placed at the north end of your garden or in a position where they won't block sunlight from smaller plants. If you're implementing a vertical garden, this could mean placing them lower down on your green wall.

Incorporate companion planting into your garden layout. This centuries-old practice involves grouping plants that benefit each other. Some plants deter pests that afflict their neighbors, while others can improve soil nutrition. For instance, marigolds can deter nematodes and other pests, while beans add nitrogen to the soil, benefiting heavy feeders like corn.

If you're using containers, think about mobility. Lightweight containers or those with wheels can be moved around to take advantage of changing sunlight conditions or to protect them from harsh weather.

Finally, remember that a garden is a dynamic, living thing. Your initial layout isn't set in stone. As you observe your garden over time, you might find that some things work better than others. Don't be afraid to make adjustments. That's part of the joy of gardening, after all. It's a constant journey of discovery, full of surprises and lessons. So, grab your pencil and paper, it's time to bring your dream garden to life!

Creating an Ornamental Garden

An ornamental garden, with its riot of colors, intoxicating scents, and intricate designs, is a joy to behold. But it's not just about beauty. An ornamental garden can also be a haven for wildlife, a soothing retreat from the hustle and bustle of city life, and a profound expression of creativity.

So, how do you create your own urban ornamental garden? Let's dive in.

Firstly, identify your purpose for creating an ornamental garden. Are you looking to attract certain wildlife, like birds or bees? Do you want a serene space for relaxation? Or is it simply an outlet for your creativity? Your purpose will guide your design choices, from the types of plants you choose to the garden layout and decorative elements.

Now, let's talk about space. As with an edible garden, a successful ornamental garden is not defined by the size of the space but how you utilize it. Even a tiny balcony can be transformed into a stunning ornamental garden with the right planning and design.

Next, consider the conditions of your garden. How much sunlight does it get? What is the quality of the soil? What is the climate like? These factors will determine the types of plants that will thrive in your garden.

Once you understand your garden conditions, it's time to choose your plants. Consider a mix of perennial plants, which live for several years, and annuals, which complete their life cycle in one year. Perennials provide structure and continuity, while annuals can be changed every year, allowing you to play with different colors and textures.

Color is a powerful tool in an ornamental garden. You might choose a monochromatic scheme, using different shades of a single color for a subtle, sophisticated look. Or you might go for a complementary color scheme, using colors that are opposite each other on the color wheel for a vibrant, dynamic effect.

Don't forget about texture and form. Varying the shape and size of your plants adds visual interest and depth to your garden. You might combine spiky plants, like ornamental grasses, with round ones, like hydrangeas, for an appealing contrast.

A well-designed garden should look good all year round. When selecting your plants, think about when they bloom and what they look like when they're not in flower. Choose a combination of plants that offer visual interest across different seasons.

Creating an ornamental garden is not just about plants. Non-living elements, like furniture, water features, and sculptures, play an essential role in the design. These elements add personality and character to your garden, making it truly your own.

And finally, an ornamental garden, like any garden, is a work in progress. Don't be afraid to experiment, to make mistakes, and to learn as you go. Gardening is a journey, not a destination. Each season brings new challenges, new opportunities, and new beauty. Embrace the process, and let it bring you joy, tranquility, and a deep connection with nature.

Developing a Wildlife-Friendly Garden

Creating a wildlife-friendly garden is a rewarding venture that not only adds to the aesthetic appeal of your urban space, but also contributes to local biodiversity. A bustling ecosystem right outside your window can be a source of endless fascination and learning, a place where you can observe the intricate web of life up close.

So, let's explore how you can transform your urban garden into a haven for local wildlife.

To start, we need to understand that a wildlife-friendly garden provides three essential things: food, water, and shelter. Incorporating these into your garden can attract a variety of creatures, from birds and butterflies to bees and beneficial insects.

For food, consider planting native species that provide nectar, pollen, seeds, berries, or nuts. Not only will these plants be more likely to thrive in your local conditions, but they'll also offer the type of nourishment local wildlife is adapted to seek. For example, plants like sunflowers and coneflowers can provide seeds for birds, while flowering plants such as lavender and salvia can offer nectar for bees and butterflies.

Water, often overlooked, is a critical component of a wildlife-friendly garden. Even a small water feature, like a birdbath or a shallow dish of water, can attract a surprising variety of wildlife. If you have the space, a small pond can provide habitat for frogs, toads, and other aquatic creatures. Remember to keep the water clean and fresh, and in colder climates, ice-free during winter.

Shelter can come in many forms. Trees and shrubs can provide nesting sites for birds and shelter for small mammals.

Log piles and leaf piles can be a haven for beneficial insects, amphibians, and hedgehogs. Consider installing birdhouses or bat boxes to provide additional shelter.

When creating your wildlife-friendly garden, diversity is key. A variety of plants with different heights, structures, and flowering times can provide food and shelter throughout the year. Also, diversity tends to attract more diversity, so the more variety you have, the more types of wildlife you're likely to see.

Avoid using chemical pesticides and fertilizers, which can harm the very creatures you're trying to attract. Instead, opt for organic methods of pest control and soil enrichment. Encourage beneficial insects, like ladybugs and lacewings, which are natural predators of many common garden pests.

Don't forget about the night-time visitors. Planting night-blooming flowers and installing bat boxes can attract nocturnal wildlife like moths and bats, adding another dimension to your wildlife garden.

Creating a wildlife-friendly garden doesn't just mean making a space for wildlife, it's also about learning to co-exist with them. This might mean tolerating a few chewed leaves in exchange for the joy of seeing butterflies flit around your garden, or learning to appreciate the role of bees and other pollinators in your garden's productivity.

In the concrete jungle of the city, a wildlife-friendly garden is a breath of fresh air. It's a place where nature thrives, where we can reconnect with the wild and learn to appreciate the beauty and complexity of the natural world.

Attracting Beneficial Insects

Beneficial insects play a critical role in maintaining the health and productivity of our gardens. From pollinating our plants to keeping pest populations in check, these unsung heroes are truly nature's little helpers. So, how can you attract and support beneficial insects in your urban garden? Let's find out.

Firstly, it's important to understand that different insects have different needs. Some are looking for nectar and pollen, others for shelter, and others for specific host plants to lay their eggs. By providing a variety of plants and habitats, you can attract a diverse range of beneficial insects.

When it comes to plant selection, diversity is key. Try to include plants of different heights, colors, and flowering times to provide a steady supply of nectar and pollen throughout the growing season. Native plants are always a good choice, as local insects have evolved to use them for food and shelter.

Flowers are the main attraction for many beneficial insects. Not only do they provide nectar and pollen, but they also serve as a hunting ground for predatory insects. Opt for plants with small, open flowers, which are more accessible to a wide range of insects. Examples include yarrow, cosmos, and sweet alyssum. Umbelliferous plants, like dill and fennel, are particularly attractive to hoverflies and parasitic wasps.

Herbs can also be a big draw for beneficial insects. Many are rich in nectar, and their strong scents can help to deter pests. Consider planting a mini herb garden with plants like lavender, rosemary, thyme, and oregano.

Certain insects, like ladybugs and lacewings, are voracious predators of garden pests, such as aphids and mites. To attract these beneficial predators, you can plant their favorite foods. For example, ladybugs are attracted to plants in the daisy family, like calendula and marigolds, while lacewings are drawn to plants with small flowers like dill, coriander, and caraway.

Provide a variety of habitats to encourage beneficial insects to take up residence in your garden. This can include a patch of wildflowers, a log pile, a rock pile, or even a specially designed insect hotel. These habitats can provide shelter, nesting sites, and overwintering sites for beneficial insects.

Avoid using chemical pesticides, which can harm beneficial insects as well as pests. If you do have a pest problem, try using organic or biological controls first.

Often, a healthy population of beneficial insects can keep pest populations in check without the need for intervention.

Lastly, remember that a little untidiness can be a good thing in a wildlife-friendly garden. A patch of nettles can provide food for butterfly caterpillars, while a pile of fallen leaves can offer shelter for overwintering insects.

Attracting beneficial insects is a fascinating aspect of gardening that allows us to work with nature, rather than against it. By creating a welcoming environment for these helpful creatures, we can enjoy a healthier, more vibrant, and more sustainable garden. So, let's open our gardens to these incredible insects and watch as they work their magic.

Creating a Bird-Friendly Garden

The presence of birds can breathe life into an urban garden, bringing movement, color, and song. But beyond their aesthetic appeal, birds also play important ecological roles, from seed dispersal to pest control. So, how can you create a garden that invites our feathered friends to visit and stay a while? Let's explore.

Just as with other wildlife, birds need three basic things from your garden: food, water, and shelter.
For food, you can provide bird feeders filled with seeds, nuts, or suet.

Different species have different dietary preferences, so a variety of foods will attract a variety of birds. However, bird feeders should be supplementary to what your garden naturally provides. Native plants that produce berries, seeds, or insects are the best choices. For example, sunflowers, coneflowers, and native berry-producing shrubs can provide a natural food source.

Water is essential for birds, not just for drinking but also for bathing. A shallow birdbath or a small pond with gently sloping sides can provide a water source. Ensure the water is clean, and change it regularly. In winter, consider a heated birdbath to provide a source of unfrozen water.

Shelter can come in the form of trees, shrubs, or a purposely built birdhouse. Native plants are often the best choices for shelter, as local bird species have evolved to nest in them. Dense shrubs or trees, climbing plants on walls or fences, and even tall grasses can provide shelter and potential nesting sites.

Nesting materials can also encourage birds to set up home in your garden. You can help them out by leaving plant clippings, straw, or even pet hair in your garden for them to find.

Birds also need safe places to perch and look out for predators. A tree with horizontal branches, a trellis, or even a simple garden stake can provide a perfect perch.

To attract a diverse range of bird species, aim for a layered garden with a mix of ground cover, medium-height shrubs, and taller trees. This mimics the natural environment where different species occupy different layers of the forest.

Try to avoid using pesticides in your garden, as these can harm birds either directly, by poisoning them, or indirectly, by reducing their food supply of insects.

Lastly, consider the specific bird species you want to attract. Different species have different needs and preferences, so do a little research to find out what your local species require.

Creating a bird-friendly garden can be a rewarding experience that brings both beauty and biodiversity to your urban space. It's a way of giving back to nature, of creating a sanctuary amid the concrete and steel of the city. So let's put out the welcome mat for our feathered friends and enjoy the vibrancy and vitality they bring to our gardens.

Building a Miniature Wildlife Pond

Water is a magnet for wildlife. Even a small pond can attract a surprising variety of creatures, from birds and bees to frogs and dragonflies. It adds a new dimension to your urban garden, both visually and ecologically. So, how can you build your own miniature wildlife pond? Let's dive in.

Firstly, choose your location. It should get plenty of sunlight, but also some shade to prevent it from overheating in the summer. The pond should be away from trees to prevent leaves from falling in and reducing the water quality. Also, consider the view from your house - you'll want to be able to see your pond and its wildlife visitors!

Next, decide on the size and shape of your pond. Even a small container or half-barrel can work if you're really tight on space. The pond should have at least one side with a gentle slope to allow creatures to easily get in and out.

Now it's time to dig. Outline the shape of your pond with a rope or a garden hose, then start digging. Remember to make the pond slightly larger than your final desired size to account for the lining.

Once you've dug your hole, check for any sharp stones or roots that might puncture the liner. You can lay a layer of sand or old carpet at the bottom to provide extra protection.

Next, install the liner. Pond liners can be bought from garden centers or online. Lay it across the hole and push it into all the corners, ensuring it's flush with the sides and bottom. Secure the edges with rocks or bricks, then slowly start filling the pond with water. The weight of the water will pull the liner into place. Trim off any excess liner, leaving a border of about 30 cm around the edge of the pond.

Now it's time to add some plants. A mix of submerged, floating, and marginal plants will help oxygenate the water, provide shelter for wildlife, and make the pond look more natural. Native plants are usually the best choice, as they're adapted to local conditions and provide suitable habitat for local wildlife.

Be sure to include a variety of habitats within the pond, such as deeper areas for overwintering creatures and shallower, marshy areas for amphibians to lay their eggs. Adding a few rocks or logs around the edges can provide basking spots for frogs and perching spots for birds. They also make the pond look more natural.

Avoid introducing fish to your wildlife pond, as they can eat smaller creatures and their eggs.

Maintenance is key to keeping your pond healthy. Remove any excess algae or fallen leaves, but leave some as they provide habitat and food for pond creatures. In autumn, you might want to cover the pond with a net to prevent leaves from falling in.

Building a miniature wildlife pond is a project that can bring immense joy and fascination. It's a window into an underwater world, a place to observe the comings and goings of a host of creatures.

It's a testament to the fact that even in a small urban garden, we can create a thriving ecosystem, a sanctuary for wildlife.

Chapter 8: Sustainable Living Beyond the Garden

Reducing Waste: Plastic-Free Gardening and Composting

As we dive into the eighth chapter of our urban gardening journey, let's open the door to a broader perspective of sustainable living.

The garden, though a small physical space, has an immense impact on our overall lifestyle. It teaches us to be mindful of our surroundings, the seasons, and the fragile balance of nature. But what if we could extend this mindfulness beyond the garden's borders and into our everyday life?

The answer lies in a conscious and responsible approach to waste management. In this chapter, we'll explore plastic-free gardening and the magic of composting, two practices that go hand in hand in creating a sustainable urban living environment.

Part I: Plastic-Free Gardening

An unavoidable reality of modern life is our reliance on plastic. It's everywhere, from our shopping bags to our gardening tools. While its convenience is undeniable, the environmental impact is equally indisputable. Plastic takes centuries to degrade, often breaking down into microplastics that end up in our soil and waterways, causing harm to wildlife and ecosystems.

The good news is that gardening offers us ample opportunities to break free from plastic dependency. By employing some creativity, a bit of elbow grease, and a commitment to sustainable practices, we can make our urban garden a model of plastic-free living.

Start by taking a good look at your gardening tools and supplies. Are there plastic pots, watering cans, or spades? If so, consider replacing them with metal, wood, or bamboo alternatives when they wear out. Natural materials are not only environmentally friendly but also add a rustic charm to your gardening routine.

When it comes to buying seeds or plants, look for vendors who use biodegradable packaging or pots. Some nurseries are now offering 'naked' seedlings that come without any packaging at all. Alternatively, consider seed swaps with local gardening groups or friends, an excellent way to reduce packaging waste and strengthen your community ties.

Mulching is another area where you can eliminate plastic. Instead of plastic sheeting, opt for organic mulches like straw, wood chips, or compost. These will not only suppress weeds but also improve soil structure and fertility over time.

Part II: Composting

Now, let's turn our attention to a sustainable practice that transforms waste into a precious garden resource: composting. Composting is nature's way of recycling. It's a process that turns organic waste, such as vegetable scraps, leaves, and grass clippings, into a nutrient-rich soil conditioner, a gardener's black gold.

Composting at home can significantly reduce the amount of waste that ends up in landfills. It's estimated that around 30% of what we throw away could be composted instead. By composting, you're not only reducing waste but also creating a valuable product that can benefit your garden.

To start composting, all you need is a small space in your garden or balcony for a compost bin or wormery. There are various types of composting methods and bins available, so you're sure to find one that suits your living situation and lifestyle.

Composting is a careful balance of green and brown materials. Green materials are rich in nitrogen and include things like vegetable scraps, coffee grounds, and fresh grass clippings. Brown materials are carbon-rich and include items such as dried leaves, straw, and shredded newspaper. A good rule of thumb is to aim for a ratio of 2:1 brown to green materials.

Turn your compost pile regularly to aid decomposition and ensure an even distribution of heat and moisture. Within a few months, you'll start to see the magic happen as your waste transforms into a rich, dark compost, teeming with life and ready to boost your garden's productivity.

The marvel of composting is that it's not just about reducing waste or creating nutrient-dense soil; it's also about fostering a closer relationship with the natural cycles of life and decay. It's about understanding that nothing in nature goes to waste, and everything has a role in the grand scheme of life.

Part III: The Broader Impact

Reducing plastic use and composting in your garden have a much wider impact than you might first imagine. As we incorporate these practices into our gardening routine, we start to see potential for waste reduction and recycling in other aspects of our lives.

In the kitchen, for instance, we can be more mindful about the packaging of the food we buy, opting for loose vegetables or items in recyclable packaging. We can choose reusable shopping bags, coffee cups, and water bottles to cut down on single-use plastics.

In the bathroom, we can switch to soap bars instead of plastic bottles, or choose companies that offer refillable containers.

Even our wardrobe choices can reflect this ethos by choosing second-hand or sustainably-produced clothing.

In essence, plastic-free living and composting are not just about making our urban gardens more sustainable. They're about making our lives more sustainable.
They invite us to reflect on our consumption habits, to make mindful choices, and to become active participants in the preservation of our planet.

Part IV: Inspiring Others

A sustainable urban garden isn't just a personal victory; it's a beacon of possibility for others. Your garden can demonstrate that plastic-free, waste-conscious living is not only feasible but also enjoyable and deeply rewarding.

So, don't be shy about your efforts. Share your experiences with friends, neighbors, and social media followers. Encourage local schools to incorporate gardening and composting into their curriculum.
Participate in community clean-up drives or set up a communal composting site in your neighborhood.

Sustainable living is about more than individual actions. It's about fostering a community that values and respects the natural world, that understands our reliance on it, and that is committed to preserving it for generations to come.

Sustainable living extends far beyond the garden, but it's in the garden where many of us can make a start. Plastic-free gardening and composting are two practices that not only enrich our gardening experience but also help us lead a more sustainable lifestyle.

As urban gardeners, we have a unique opportunity to make a real difference, to turn our small spaces into examples of sustainable living, and inspire others to do the same. Let's make the most of it.

Water Conservation: Rainwater Harvesting and Efficient Watering

Underneath the umbrella of sustainable living, water conservation is another significant aspect that we, as responsible urban gardeners, need to consider. Water is a precious resource that often gets overlooked due to its apparent abundance, but its judicious use is vital for maintaining a sustainable balance in our environment. In this section, we will delve into rainwater harvesting and efficient watering methods, two key strategies that can help you make every drop count.

Part I: Rainwater Harvesting

The concept of rainwater harvesting isn't new; it's been practiced for centuries by civilizations around the world. Today, amidst our densely populated cities and changing climate patterns, it remains a highly effective and eco-friendly method of water conservation.

Rainwater harvesting is simply the collection and storage of rainwater for later use. For the urban gardener, this means capturing the rain that falls on your roof, balcony, or patio and using it to water your plants. This practice not only conserves water but also reduces stormwater runoff, which can lead to erosion and water pollution.

You can start harvesting rainwater by installing a rain barrel at the end of a downspout or beneath a drainpipe. These barrels come in various sizes to suit different spaces and can be discreetly tucked away. Some modern designs even incorporate planters on top, making them both practical and aesthetically pleasing.

The water you collect is free from the chemicals often found in tap water, such as chlorine, which makes it better for your plants. It's worth noting, however, that rainwater collected in urban areas may contain pollutants from the atmosphere or roof surfaces, so it's best used for ornamental plants rather than edible crops.

Part II: Efficient Watering

While collecting rainwater is a proactive step towards water conservation, it's equally important to ensure we're using water efficiently in our gardens. Many of us, with the best intentions at heart, end up overwatering our plants.

Not only does this waste water, but it can also be detrimental to plant health.

The first step towards efficient watering is understanding your plants' needs. Different plants have different water requirements depending on their species, size, and stage of growth. As a general rule, it's better to water deeply and infrequently, encouraging plants to develop deep root systems that make them more resilient and water-efficient.

Next, consider the timing of your watering. The early morning or late evening is the best time to water your plants as it reduces evaporation. Avoid watering in the heat of the day when most of the water would be lost to evaporation before it even reaches the plant roots.

Mulching is another valuable practice for efficient watering. Covering the soil around your plants with a layer of organic material, such as compost, straw, or wood chips, helps retain moisture, suppress weeds, and add nutrients to the soil.

Drip irrigation systems can also be a worthwhile investment for the urban gardener. These systems deliver water directly to the base of the plant, minimizing evaporation and reducing the spread of waterborne diseases.

Water conservation is an integral part of sustainable urban gardening. By implementing practices such as rainwater harvesting and efficient watering, we can make the most of every drop, benefiting our gardens, our community, and the planet. It's yet another step towards extending the sustainability of our gardens into our broader lifestyle, another piece of the puzzle in our quest for responsible, mindful living.

Supporting Local Food Systems: Community Gardens and Farmers' Markets

In our exploration of sustainable living beyond the garden, it's important to acknowledge the broader food system that we're a part of. Our individual efforts to grow food at home can contribute to a larger movement towards local, sustainable food systems. In this section, we'll discuss the role of community gardens and farmers' markets, two vital components of local food systems that have the potential to transform the way we eat and live.

Part I: Community Gardens

Community gardens are shared spaces where people come together to grow food, flowers, and other plants. These gardens can be found in a variety of urban settings, from vacant lots to rooftops, and they offer an array of benefits for both individuals and the community at large.

On a personal level, community gardens provide access to fresh, locally grown food, often in areas where it's otherwise hard to come by. They offer a chance to learn about gardening, share knowledge, and foster a sense of accomplishment as you watch your plants grow and thrive.

On a community level, these gardens can transform underutilized spaces into vibrant, green areas that provide habitat for local wildlife and improve air quality. They can serve as a gathering place, strengthening community bonds and promoting a sense of shared responsibility for our environment.

If you have the opportunity to join or start a community garden, it's an excellent way to expand your gardening activities beyond your personal space and make a broader impact in your neighborhood.

Part II: Farmers' Markets

Farmers' markets are another cornerstone of local food systems. They provide a platform for farmers and food producers to sell directly to consumers, cutting out the middleman and fostering a closer connection between people and the food they eat.

Purchasing food from farmers' markets supports local agriculture and reduces the environmental impact of food transport. The food you find at these markets is typically fresher and more diverse than what's available at conventional supermarkets, reflecting the local growing season and showcasing varieties that aren't typically found in larger retail outlets.

Farmers' markets are also a rich source of knowledge. Farmers are often eager to share information about their products, offering tips on preparing, storing, and even growing your own. This connection to our food and the people who grow it can inspire us to make more sustainable choices in our own gardens and kitchens.

By supporting community gardens and farmers' markets, we are not just improving our personal access to fresh, local food. We are also contributing to a more sustainable and resilient local food system. We're voting with our dollars and our time for a system that values community, environmental stewardship, and the simple pleasure of good food grown close to home.

Remember, sustainable living is about more than the actions we take as individuals. It's about the communities we build, the systems we support, and the world we envision. By extending the principles of sustainability from our personal gardens to our local food systems, we can help create a world that's more connected, more resilient, and more in tune with the rhythms of nature.

Reducing Waste in Your Garden

As we navigate our way towards sustainable living, it's crucial to tackle an aspect that is often overlooked but bears tremendous impact - waste production in our garden. Surprisingly, even in our green spaces, waste can accumulate. From plant trimmings to packaging from garden supplies, waste can start to pile up if not managed consciously. In this section, we'll explore how we can transform our urban gardens into zero-waste spaces.

Part I: Garden Waste

One of the most common types of waste in a garden is organic waste. This includes fallen leaves, grass clippings, spent flowers, and vegetable scraps. Instead of viewing these materials as waste, we should view them as resources.

As we learned earlier, composting is a fantastic way to turn organic waste into a valuable soil amendment. Composting not only reduces the amount of waste going to the landfill but also enriches your garden soil, improving its structure, fertility, and ability to hold water.

Another option for dealing with garden waste is creating a wildlife pile. Stack woody prunings and branches in a quiet corner of your garden to create a habitat for beneficial insects, small mammals, and birds. This not only recycles your garden waste but also increases biodiversity in your garden.

Part II: Packaging Waste

Packaging from garden supplies like seeds, pots, and tools can contribute significantly to waste. To reduce this, opt for suppliers who use minimal and environmentally friendly packaging. Consider buying in bulk where possible to reduce packaging waste.

When it comes to plant pots, opt for biodegradable or reusable options. Many garden centers now accept plastic pots for recycling, so take advantage of these schemes where available. Better yet, get creative and repurpose items around your home into unique plant containers.

Part III: Water Waste

Water is a precious resource, and wasting it is a common issue in many gardens. We've already discussed the importance of rainwater harvesting and efficient watering techniques in reducing water waste.

Another strategy is choosing drought-tolerant plants or native species that are adapted to your local climate conditions. These plants require less water and are often more resistant to pests and diseases, reducing the need for chemical interventions.

Part IV: Material Waste

Finally, consider the materials used in your garden structures and decorations. Opt for durable, sustainably sourced materials that will withstand the elements and age gracefully. When these materials eventually come to the end of their lives, consider if they can be repurposed before being disposed of.

Reducing waste in your garden is a journey, not a destination. It requires a shift in perspective, from viewing waste as something to be discarded to seeing it as a resource to be utilized.

It's an ongoing process of learning, experimenting, and refining your practices. But the rewards - a healthier garden, a lighter ecological footprint, and the satisfaction of aligning your actions with your values - are well worth the effort.

Chapter 9: Case Studies and Success Stories

Inspiring Examples of Urban Gardens Around the World

If you've been following along with us in this urban gardening journey, you're probably eager to see some real-life examples of how these principles and practices have been put into action.
This chapter is your ticket to a world tour of urban gardens. Each has its own unique story, filled with the triumphs and tribulations that are inherent to urban gardening.

Let's begin our journey in the buzzing heart of New York City, with an inspiring venture known as the Battery Urban Farm. This one-acre educational farm located in Battery Park was initiated in 2011 by the Battery Conservancy to educate, engage, and inspire New Yorkers about sustainable farming.

They grow over a hundred varieties of organically-grown vegetables, fruits, flowers, grains, and companion plants. Not only has it become a thriving, biodiverse oasis in the concrete jungle, but it has also proven to be a powerful educational tool for thousands of students and teachers from around the city.

Journeying across the Pacific, we land in Japan, where a creative approach to urban gardening, Machikado Bāsai, has taken root. Translating to "street-side farming," this is a movement where homeowners convert the street-facing edges of their property into productive mini-farms. These slivers of land, often just a few feet wide, are turned into lush, green spaces, growing everything from herbs and leafy greens to fruit-bearing trees. The initiative not only provides residents with fresh produce but also adds a touch of nature to the concrete and steel cities.

Next, we'll travel to London, where the Skip Garden has been making waves. As the name implies, this community project creatively repurposes old skips (dumpsters) into thriving vegetable patches. But that's not all. They also utilize other upcycled materials like construction waste and office furniture to create their growing spaces. The Skip Garden is more than an urban farm—it's a statement on sustainability and resourcefulness in a rapidly urbanizing world.

Heading south to the vibrant city of Havana, Cuba, we find the Organopónicos. These are a system of urban organic gardens developed in the wake of the dissolution of the Soviet Union, which caused severe food and fertilizer shortages. These community-run gardens, often nestled between city buildings or on unused plots, have played a significant role in boosting local food security and promoting organic agriculture.

Organopónicos are a testament to the resilience and resourcefulness of urban gardeners in the face of adversity.

Our final destination takes us to the African continent, to the city of Nairobi, Kenya, where vertical sack gardening is transforming urban food production. With limited space in the city's densely populated areas, residents have taken to growing vegetables in vertically-stacked sacks filled with soil. This ingenious solution not only maximizes space but also requires less water than traditional gardening methods.

These are just a few examples of the remarkable work being done by urban gardeners worldwide. Each of these projects, in their own unique way, is helping to redefine what it means to garden in the city. They show us that the challenges of urban spaces—limited space, poor soil, lack of green areas—can be overcome with creativity, resourcefulness, and a touch of green-fingered magic.

The stories of these urban gardens are not just about growing plants; they're about growing communities, improving lives, and, ultimately, changing the world—one garden at a time.

So, as we continue our urban gardening journey, let these success stories inspire you and remind you of the immense possibilities that await in your own urban garden.

Interviews with Successful Urban Gardeners

An urban garden, much like a traditional one, is a canvas for the gardener's creativity and passion. It's a symphony of nature where every plant, every insect, and every handful of soil plays a part. And who better to shed light on this beautiful harmony than the maestros themselves—the successful urban gardeners who have nurtured these spaces to life.

Let's meet some of these inspiring individuals. (Their full names have been withheld out of respect for their privacy).

Our first interviewee is Fatima, the powerhouse behind a community garden in Detroit, Michigan. Once a barren lot, the space now flourishes with vegetables, herbs, and flowers.

Fatima's love for gardening was ignited during her childhood in rural Alabama, and she brought that passion to her urban home. "The secret," she says, "is to see potential where others see none. An empty lot, a rooftop, a balcony—it's all potential garden space. All it needs is some love, care, and good compost."

Next, we chat with Akio, a key figure in Tokyo's Machikado Bāsai movement. A retired teacher, Akio has transformed the sidewalk outside his house into a lush green space, teeming with plants.

"It's not just about the plants," Akio tells us. "It's about the community. My little garden has become a gathering place for neighbors. We share tips, seeds, and, of course, the harvest. It's brought us closer together."

Then we meet Jenny, the brains behind the Skip Garden in London.

As a landscape architect, Jenny saw the potential in discarded items and turned them into thriving mini gardens. "The challenge of urban gardening," she shares, "is also its charm. Yes, space is limited, and soil may be poor, but that just fuels creativity. And the satisfaction of seeing things grow in the heart of the city—it's priceless."

Our journey takes us next to Havana, where we sit down with Carlos, a seasoned member of the local Organopónicos.

Carlos and his community have worked wonders with their urban gardens, turning adversity into opportunity. "Our gardens have taught us resilience," Carlos says. "We don't have fancy equipment or fertilizers, but we have each other. We've learned to work with nature, not against it. And in return, it has given us food, green spaces, and a sense of pride."

Finally, we head to Nairobi, where we meet Grace, an innovator in vertical sack gardening.

Grace's ingenuity has turned her modest home into a verdant oasis, inspiring many in her community. "Don't wait for the perfect conditions," she advises. "Start small, start now. You'll make mistakes, sure. But you'll also watch life grow from your hands. There's no feeling quite like it."

Each of these urban gardeners, with their unique journeys, offers invaluable insights into the world of urban gardening. They remind us that successful gardening is not just about the right tools or techniques.

It's about passion, community, resilience, creativity, and the sheer joy of nurturing life. These gardeners are not just growing plants—they are sowing seeds of change, one urban garden at a time.

Lessons Learned and Tips for Success

The world of urban gardening is as diverse as the cities we inhabit, each garden a distinct testament to the power of nature in urban spaces. From our case studies and interviews with successful urban gardeners, several key lessons emerge that can guide new and experienced gardeners alike.

1. **See Potential Everywhere**: The first step in urban gardening is to perceive the potential in your

space, regardless of its size or state. As Fatima from Detroit demonstrated, an empty lot, a balcony, even a sidewalk can be transformed into a thriving garden. It's all about seeing the possibilities.
2. **Build Community**: Urban gardens are about more than plants—they're about people. As Akio from Tokyo found, a garden can become a gathering place, fostering a sense of community and shared purpose. So, don't just plant seeds, plant relationships. Share tips, swap seeds, and celebrate the harvest together.
3. **Embrace Creativity**: Limited space and resources in urban environments can actually stimulate creativity. Jenny from the Skip Garden showed us that with a little imagination, waste materials can become valuable assets in the garden. So, look around, and you might be surprised at what can be repurposed for your garden.
4. **Resilience is Key**: Urban gardening isn't always smooth sailing. There can be challenges, from poor soil to scarce water supply. But as Carlos from Havana taught us, these obstacles can be overcome with resilience and cooperation. Keep learning, keep adapting, and remember: every challenge is an opportunity in disguise.
5. **Start Now, Start Small**: Don't wait for the perfect conditions—they rarely exist. Instead, take a page from Grace's book in Nairobi and start small, start now. Even a single pot of herbs is a step in the right direction. Learn as you go, and don't be afraid to make mistakes. They're part of the process.

6. **Respect Nature**: Above all, successful urban gardening involves working with nature, not against it. This means understanding the needs of your plants, the condition of your soil, and the local climate. Use organic methods whenever possible, and aim to create a balanced, biodiverse garden that will attract beneficial insects and promote a healthy growing environment.

Remember, every garden is unique, and every gardener's journey is different. What works for one garden might not work for another. The real secret to success lies in patience, observation, and a willingness to learn.

So take these lessons, apply them to your garden, and watch as your urban oasis grows.

Best Practices for Harvesting

After weeks of tender care and patient nurturing, there's nothing quite as rewarding as the moment when you get to harvest your own home-grown produce. Yet, as any seasoned gardener will tell you, harvesting is more than just plucking produce off the plant. It's an art, and there are best practices to ensure you do it right. Here, we'll share some of the most important ones.

1. **Timing is Everything**: Knowing when to harvest can greatly affect the taste, texture, and nutritional content of your produce. Some plants, like zucchini

or peas, are best harvested young, when they are tender and sweet. Others, like tomatoes and peppers, need to fully ripen on the plant for maximum flavor. Research your specific plants and understand their ideal harvesting stage. Remember, observation is key!

2. **Use the Right Tools**: For some plants, a simple twist and pull will do the job, but others may require a pair of pruners or a knife. Using the right tool can prevent unnecessary damage to the plant, which could invite disease or inhibit further growth. Always ensure your tools are clean and sharp to avoid spreading disease.

3. **Harvest Regularly**: Many plants, like beans, tomatoes, and herbs, will produce more if they are harvested frequently. Regular harvesting signals to the plant that it needs to keep producing. Also, overripe fruits and vegetables can attract pests, so regular harvesting helps keep your plants healthier.

4. **Handle with Care**: Remember, freshly harvested produce is delicate. Handle your harvest gently to avoid bruising or damaging the produce. This is especially important for fruits like tomatoes and peaches, which can easily be damaged by rough handling.

5. **Store Properly**: Once harvested, proper storage is key to maintaining the quality of your produce. Most fruits and vegetables should be stored in a cool, dark place to prolong their freshness. Some produce, like tomatoes and bananas, produce

ethylene gas, which can speed up the ripening (and subsequent spoilage) of nearby produce. Store these separately to avoid premature spoilage.
6. **Share the Bounty**: Finally, don't forget the community aspect of urban gardening. If you find yourself with more produce than you can consume, consider sharing it with your neighbors, friends, or a local food bank. As our interviewees have shown, urban gardening isn't just about growing food—it's about fostering community.

Harvesting is the culmination of your gardening efforts, the moment when you get to reap the fruits (or vegetables, herbs, or grains) of your labor.

By following these best practices, you can ensure that you get the most out of your harvest, both in terms of quantity and quality. Happy harvesting!

Preserving and Storing Your Produce

The joy of urban gardening doesn't end with the harvest. In fact, one of the most satisfying aspects of growing your own food is enjoying your home-grown produce long after the growing season has ended. This is where proper preservation and storage come into play.

Here, we'll explore some best practices for preserving and storing your urban garden's bounty.

1. Storing Fresh Produce

Each type of produce has its own storage needs, and understanding these can greatly extend the shelf-life of your harvest.

- Root vegetables like carrots and potatoes prefer cool, dark, and humid conditions. A basement or cellar can often provide the perfect environment.
- Many fruits and vegetables, such as tomatoes, citrus fruits, and peppers, should be stored at room temperature, away from direct sunlight.
- Leafy greens, broccoli, and berries do best in the high-humidity crisper drawer of your refrigerator.

Remember to always handle your fresh produce gently to prevent bruising, and inspect regularly for signs of spoilage—remember, one bad apple can indeed spoil the whole bunch!

2. Freezing

Freezing is a simple and effective way to preserve many types of fruits and vegetables. Berries, peas, corn, and chopped leafy greens often freeze well. To freeze, spread the produce in a single layer on a baking sheet, freeze until solid, and then transfer to airtight containers or freezer bags.

3. Canning

Canning is another excellent way to preserve your harvest. There are two main methods: water bath canning, suitable for high-acid foods like jams, jellies, and pickles; and pressure canning, necessary for low-acid foods like vegetables and meats. Canning can seem intimidating at first, but with a bit of practice, it can be a rewarding and even fun process.

4. Drying
Drying, either in a low oven, a dehydrator, or even in the sun, is a traditional way to preserve fruits, vegetables, and herbs. Dried produce can be used in cooking, baking, or as a tasty snack.

5. Pickling and Fermenting
Pickling and fermenting not only preserve your produce but also can enhance their nutritional value. From classic dill pickles to tangy sauerkraut and spicy kimchi, the possibilities are nearly endless.

6. Root Cellaring
For those with a bit more space, a root cellar can be an effective way to store large quantities of produce. Root cellars take advantage of cool, moist underground conditions to keep produce fresh for months.

Remember, the key to successful preservation is starting with high-quality, freshly harvested produce. So, don't wait until your harvest is past its prime—start preserving while your produce is at its freshest and most flavorful.

By preserving and storing your harvest properly, you can enjoy the fruits of your labor year-round.

Enjoying Your Harvest: Simple Recipes and Ideas

Harvesting your own produce is a delight, but the real magic happens when you bring your harvest into the kitchen. The fresh, vibrant flavors of home-grown fruits, vegetables, and herbs can truly shine in simple, thoughtfully prepared dishes.

Here, we'll share a few recipes and ideas that celebrate the fruits of your labor.

1. Fresh Tomato Bruschetta
This classic Italian dish is a perfect way to enjoy ripe, home-grown tomatoes. Simply dice your tomatoes, add a clove of minced garlic, a handful of finely chopped basil, a drizzle of good quality olive oil, and a sprinkle of sea salt. Mix together and spoon onto slices of toasted baguette. It's a taste of summer in every bite!

2. Garden Green Smoothie
For a healthy start to your day, why not whip up a green smoothie using leafy greens from your garden? Blend a handful of spinach or kale, a ripe banana, a cup of almond milk, and a tablespoon of honey or agave syrup. For an extra health boost, add a spoonful of chia seeds or a scoop of your favorite protein powder.

3. Roasted Root Vegetables

There's nothing quite like the sweet, earthy flavor of roasted root vegetables. Simply chop a mix of your favorite roots—carrots, beets, potatoes, parsnips—toss them in olive oil, salt, and your favorite herbs, then roast in a hot oven until tender and caramelized.

4. Fresh Herb Pesto

If you find yourself with an abundance of herbs, why not make a pesto? Traditional pesto is made with basil, but feel free to experiment with whatever you have on hand. Simply blend together two cups of fresh herbs, a half cup of nuts (pine nuts, almonds, or walnuts work well), a half cup of grated parmesan cheese, and about a half cup of olive oil. It's delicious on pasta, spread on sandwiches, or used as a marinade.

5. Pickled Vegetables

Pickling is a great way to preserve your harvest and enjoy it throughout the year. Try quick-pickling a mix of veggies like cucumbers, carrots, radishes, or green beans. All you need is a simple brine made from vinegar, water, sugar, and salt, and a few jars to store your pickles.

6. Garden Fresh Salsa

There's nothing quite like salsa made from fresh, garden-ripened tomatoes. Dice up a couple of tomatoes, a jalapeño (or more, depending on how spicy you like your salsa), and a small onion. Add a squeeze of lime juice, a handful of chopped cilantro, and a dash of salt. Perfect for taco night or just with some tortilla chips!

7. Hearty Vegetable Soup

This is an excellent way to use up a surplus of vegetables and create a comforting, healthy meal. Start with a base of sautéed onions, carrots, and celery. Add in diced vegetables of your choice (think potatoes, zucchini, green beans, peas) and a can of diced tomatoes. Cover with vegetable broth and let simmer until all the vegetables are tender. Add herbs like thyme, rosemary, or basil for extra flavor.

8. Zucchini Bread

When zucchini season hits, it hits hard. If you're looking for a way to use up zucchini, baking is a surprisingly delicious option. Shredded zucchini can be incorporated into breads and muffins, adding moisture and a slight sweetness that pairs wonderfully with spices like cinnamon and nutmeg.

9. Infused Oils and Vinegars

This is a great way to capture the flavor of fresh herbs and it couldn't be simpler. For infused oils, gently heat a cup of oil (like olive or canola) with a handful of your favorite herbs. Let it cool, then strain out the herbs. For infused vinegars, simply place the herbs in a jar, cover with vinegar, and let it sit for a few weeks before straining. These make for beautiful gifts as well!

10. Grilled Veggie Kabobs

Take advantage of the barbecue season and throw some home-grown veggies on the grill. Chunky pieces of bell pepper, zucchini, mushrooms, and onions work well. Marinate them in a mix of olive oil, lemon juice, garlic, and your favorite herbs, then thread onto skewers. Grill until charred and tender.

These are just a few ideas to get you started. The possibilities are truly endless when you're cooking with home-grown produce.

Remember, one of the joys of growing your own food is the freedom to experiment and explore. So, don't be afraid to try new recipes, play around with different flavor combinations, and most importantly, enjoy the process. Let the quality of your home-grown produce shine through.

And don't forget to share! Sharing the bounty of your garden with friends, family, and neighbors is one of the greatest joys of urban gardening.

Chapter 10: Moving Forward: Expanding Your Urban Garden

Taking Your Urban Garden to the Next Level

So, you've tilled your first tiny plot, planted your seedlings, watched them sprout, grow, and bear fruit. You've tasted the sweet reward of your labor and enjoyed the lush greenery in your urban space. Your urban garden, though small, is a source of pride and joy. But the allure of the garden is such that once you dip your toes into it, you yearn to wade deeper.

The question then arises, how can you take your urban garden to the next level? This chapter is dedicated to those ready to expand their horizon and undertake the exhilarating challenge of transforming their compact urban oasis into a more flourishing, productive, and vibrant space.

1. Maximize Your Space

Urban gardens often suffer from one primary constraint - space. But with a little ingenuity, you can make every inch count. Consider vertical gardening techniques like trellises, hanging baskets, or green walls. They not only offer a great way to grow vines, climbers, or cascading plants but also add visual interest to your garden.

Don't overlook the potential of unconventional spaces such as balconies, window sills, rooftops, or even the side of a sunny wall. With the right containers and suitable plants, these spaces can burst into a riot of greenery. Remember, the goal is to see possibility, not limitation.

2. Expand Your Plant Palette

One of the most exciting aspects of expanding your urban garden is the chance to diversify your plant selection. Perhaps you've been growing herbs and lettuces, but now you could try your hand at root vegetables or dwarf fruit trees. Experiment with different varieties of the same vegetable.

Try a rainbow of tomatoes, a symphony of peppers, or a dance of beans. You could introduce aromatic herbs that serve dual purposes as pest deterrents and culinary stars.

Expanding your plant repertoire also allows you to create a more balanced and sustainable garden. Companion planting, the practice of planting different crops in proximity for pest control, pollination, providing habitat for beneficial insects, maximizing use of space, and to otherwise increase crop productivity, is a wonderful technique to explore.

3. Incorporating Permaculture Principles

Permaculture principles can significantly contribute to the productivity and sustainability of your urban garden. These principles focus on designing gardens that mimic the patterns observed in natural ecosystems. They include concepts like designing from patterns to details, using and valuing diversity, integrating rather than segregating, and using edges and valuing the marginal.

For instance, by integrating rather than segregating, you can build a mini ecosystem where each plant serves multiple purposes. A tall sunflower provides shade for lettuce, acts as a trellis for beans, and once it goes to seed, becomes a food source for birds.

4. Embracing Technology

Don't shy away from using technology in your urban garden. From automatic irrigation systems to indoor grow lights, technology can help you overcome many urban gardening challenges. You might consider installing a simple drip irrigation system for water efficiency or try out a gardening app to help keep track of planting times and pest control schedules.

5. Education and Community Engagement

Gardening, at its heart, is a journey of continuous learning. As you expand your garden, invest time in learning about soil health, composting, organic pest control, and other such topics. Attend workshops, join local gardening clubs, and engage with the online gardening community.

6. Seasonal Planning and Crop Rotation

As your urban garden expands, planning becomes more crucial. Make sure to plan your garden according to the seasons. This not only includes knowing when to plant certain crops, but also understanding how changing sunlight, temperature, and rainfall patterns could affect your garden.

Crop rotation, or the practice of growing different types of crops in the same area across different seasons, is another technique you can incorporate into your garden. This can help prevent the buildup of pests and diseases that tend to afflict specific crop types, while also helping to improve soil fertility and structure.

7. Creating a Wildlife-Friendly Garden

While an urban garden might not seem like the ideal place for wildlife, with a little effort, you can turn it into a haven for beneficial insects, birds, and even small mammals. Consider installing bird feeders or bird baths, planting native plants to attract local insects and bees, and creating small habitats for beneficial creatures like ladybugs, spiders, and worms. Creating a wildlife-friendly garden not only contributes to local biodiversity but also aids in natural pest control.

8. Expanding Into Aquaponics or Hydroponics

If you're ready for a new challenge and have a bit more space and resources, consider venturing into aquaponics or hydroponics. Both these methods allow you to grow plants without soil, making them ideal for urban spaces where soil quality might be a concern. Aquaponics even lets you raise fish, which can be a great source of protein for your household.

9. Composting and Soil Health

As your garden grows, so will your responsibility towards maintaining soil health. Composting your kitchen waste is a great way to produce nutrient-rich compost for your plants. It also contributes to a circular economy where waste is not wasted but utilized efficiently. Learn about different composting techniques and find one that fits your urban setting and lifestyle.

10. Aesthetics and Personal Touch

Last, but not least, never forget that your garden is an extension of your home and your personality. As you expand, ensure that it remains a place of beauty, comfort, and joy. Whether you love a wild, bohemian look, or a neat, minimalist design, your garden should reflect your aesthetic taste. Add personal touches like garden ornaments, a reading corner, or maybe even a small garden gnome hiding amongst the foliage.

Taking your urban garden to the next level doesn't necessarily mean you need a large space or a big budget.

It's more about creativity, resourcefulness, and a willingness to experiment and learn. The expanded garden will not only yield more produce, but it will also provide more opportunities for learning, for experiencing nature, and for creating a sustainable lifestyle in the heart of the city.

The journey might be challenging, but the rewards are worth every drop of sweat and every speck of dirt under your nails.

Engaging the Community in Urban Gardening

Community is at the heart of gardening. Beyond the humble plot that you call your own, gardening can serve as a powerful connector of people, fostering relationships, encouraging mutual learning, and promoting a shared responsibility towards our environment. Engaging your community in urban gardening brings these benefits to a local level, transforming isolated efforts into a vibrant, collective endeavor.

1. Sharing Your Garden
You don't need to host a grand garden party (although you certainly can!) to share your garden. Simply inviting your neighbors, friends, or family to see your green space can

spark conversations, inspire others to start their own gardening journey, and even initiate exchanges of ideas, plants, or harvests. Your garden, no matter how small, can become a hub of connection and learning.

2. Starting a Community Garden

If you have access to a larger plot of unused land - maybe a vacant lot, a public park, or even a rooftop, consider starting a community garden. Community gardens offer a space where people can come together to grow food, flowers, and friendships.

They can serve as living classrooms, teaching not only gardening techniques but also important values like teamwork, respect for nature, and food security.

As a seasoned urban gardener, you could spearhead such an initiative or play a leading role in managing and organizing it.

3. Organizing Workshops and Demos

Sharing your gardening knowledge can go a long way in promoting urban gardening in your community. Consider organizing workshops or demonstrations on topics you're familiar with.

It could be a practical demo on making compost, a fun workshop on container gardening, or a talk on the benefits of growing your own food.

If you're not comfortable conducting these sessions alone, you could team up with local gardening clubs or invite other gardening enthusiasts to join you.

4. Collaborating with Local Schools

Schools are excellent places to engage the community in urban gardening. Initiating a garden-based learning program can help children understand where their food comes from, appreciate the importance of healthy eating, and develop a sense of responsibility towards the environment.

As an experienced urban gardener, you could volunteer to set up and maintain a school garden, offer hands-on classes, or guide teachers on incorporating the garden into their curriculum.

5. Encouraging Citizen Science

Citizen science projects are a great way to engage the community in urban gardening while contributing to scientific knowledge.

Whether it's monitoring local pollinators, observing seasonal changes in plants, or recording bird species visiting your garden, these projects can enrich your gardening experience and connect you with a broader community of citizen scientists.

Sharing such initiatives with your neighbors or friends can spark their interest in gardening and its wider implications.

6. Setting Up a Garden Produce Swap

Imagine a place where homegrown tomatoes can be exchanged for fresh basil, where surplus zucchini finds a home, and where the fruits of everyone's labor are shared and enjoyed.

A community produce swap does just this, promoting not only the distribution of fresh, local food but also the sharing of gardening tips, recipes, and experiences.
As an urban gardener, you can organize such swaps and turn them into eagerly anticipated, regular community events.

Engaging the community in urban gardening requires effort, but the rewards are manifold. The shared sense of accomplishment, the collective learning, and the strengthened bonds between neighbors make every effort worthwhile. Plus, it's always more fun to garden together, isn't it?

Urban Gardening and Its Impact on Mental and Physical Health

Urban gardening, with its lush greenery and colorful produce, isn't just a feast for the eyes and palate. It also serves as a powerful panacea for the body and mind.

The act of tending to plants, from sowing seeds to harvesting crops, has profound benefits for our physical and mental health, making urban gardening not just a hobby, but a holistic wellness practice.

1. Physical Health Benefits

Engaging in regular gardening activities is a great way to maintain and improve physical health.

Exercise: Gardening involves a fair bit of physical work. Digging, planting, weeding, watering, and harvesting are all activities that can contribute to your daily dose of moderate-intensity exercise. From improving cardiovascular health to strengthening muscles and increasing flexibility, the physical work involved in gardening can help keep you fit and active.

Nutrition: Growing your own food in an urban garden can greatly enhance your nutritional intake. You have direct access to fresh, organic produce, free from harmful pesticides and preservatives. You can harvest your fruits and vegetables at their peak ripeness, ensuring maximum nutrient content. Plus, the joy of eating something you've grown yourself often leads to increased consumption of fruits and vegetables, further boosting your dietary health.

2. Mental Health Benefits

Urban gardening's influence extends far beyond the physical, with numerous benefits for mental and emotional health.

Stress Relief: Gardens are known to be tranquil spaces, offering a respite from the hustle and bustle of urban life. The simple act of tending to plants can be therapeutic, reducing stress levels and promoting relaxation. Studies have shown that gardening can lower cortisol levels, a hormone often associated with stress, and improve mood.

***Mindfulness*:** Gardening is a mindful activity. It encourages you to be present in the moment, focusing on the task at hand, whether it's sowing seeds, pruning leaves, or simply observing the subtle changes in your plants. This form of mindfulness can help reduce symptoms of anxiety and depression, improve attention and focus, and enhance overall mental well-being.

***Sense of Accomplishment*:** Watching a seed you planted grow into a flourishing plant and yield produce can bring a deep sense of satisfaction and accomplishment. These positive feelings can bolster self-esteem and contribute to a more positive outlook on life.

3. Community and Social Health

While gardening can be a solitary activity, it can also foster a sense of community when done collectively.

***Social Interaction*:** Community gardens or shared gardening projects can serve as social hubs, encouraging interaction between people of different ages, backgrounds, and walks of life. These interactions can reduce feelings of isolation, promote a sense of belonging, and contribute to improved social well-being.

***Educational Opportunities*:** Urban gardening offers plenty of opportunities for learning, which can stimulate mental activity and encourage lifelong learning. Whether it's learning about different plant species, understanding the basics of composting, or experimenting with vertical gardening, the educational aspect of gardening can contribute to cognitive health.

The humble act of urban gardening can play a significant role in promoting mental and physical health. It's a holistic practice that nourishes the body, soothes the mind, and nurtures the soul.

So the next time you're in your garden, remember - every seed you sow is not just a potential plant, but also a step towards better health and well-being.

Experimenting with New Plants

There is a certain comfort in growing what you know. Those familiar plants that have shared your urban garden space, season after season, can become like old friends. But just as meeting new people can bring fresh perspectives and enrich our lives, experimenting with new plants can infuse vitality and intrigue into our urban gardens.

1. Venturing Beyond the Comfort Zone
The first step to experimenting with new plants is embracing the spirit of adventure. This doesn't mean you need to bid farewell to your favorite plants. Instead, allocate a portion of your garden or a few containers where you will sow your new experiments.

2. Selecting the Right Plants

Deciding which new plants to grow can be a delightful challenge. The world of plants is vast and varied, offering a dazzling array of possibilities.

Edibles: If you've been growing herbs and leafy greens, perhaps it's time to try root vegetables like beets or radishes, or fruiting crops like tomatoes or peppers. If space allows, you could even try dwarf fruit trees or berry bushes.

Flowers: Flowers can bring color, fragrance, and pollinators to your garden. If you're new to flowers, start with easy-to-grow options like marigolds, petunias, or sunflowers. Then, you could progress to more exotic species or try your hand at perennial flowers.

Succulents and Cacti: These hardy plants can bring a different aesthetic to your garden. Plus, they're low maintenance and excellent for containers, making them perfect for an urban garden setting.

Native Plants: Native plants can be a wonderful addition to your garden. They're adapted to your local climate and soil conditions, and can attract local wildlife like birds and beneficial insects.

3. Research and Planning

Before you plant your new seeds or seedlings, spend some time researching their specific needs. Understanding the sunlight, water, soil, and space requirements of your new plants can help ensure a successful venture into the unfamiliar.

Also, consider how these new plants will fit into your existing garden. Some might require trellises or support, others might prefer the company of specific companion plants, and some might need to be protected from pests or harsh weather conditions.

4. Embrace Failure as a Learning Opportunity
When you're experimenting with new plants, not all will thrive. And that's perfectly fine. Each failed attempt is an opportunity to learn - about the plant, about your garden, and about your own gardening skills. Remember, even the most experienced gardeners have their share of failed experiments.

5. Record Your Experiences
Maintaining a garden journal can be extremely beneficial when you're trying new plants. Record your observations, track your plants' progress, note down any issues and how you addressed them. Over time, this journal can become a valuable resource, guiding your future experiments and helping you become a more versatile and knowledgeable urban gardener.

Experimenting with new plants can enrich your gardening experience in many ways. It can challenge you, teach you, surprise you, and reward you in the most unexpected ways.

So go ahead, explore the fascinating world of plants, and let your urban garden be a testament to your botanical adventures.

Advanced Hydroponics and Aquaponics

As you grow more confident in your urban gardening skills and begin looking for new challenges, you might want to delve into the fascinating world of soilless agriculture – hydroponics and aquaponics.
Both methods present advanced and sustainable ways to maximize the potential of your limited urban space, while minimizing water usage and eliminating soil-borne diseases.

1. Exploring Hydroponics
Hydroponics is a method of growing plants without soil, instead using mineral nutrient solutions in a water solvent. Hydroponic systems can be set up in various ways, depending on your space availability, plant choices, and technical skills.

***Types of Hydroponic Systems*:** Some common hydroponic systems include the wick system (the simplest type), deepwater culture (DWC), nutrient film technique (NFT), ebb and flow (flood and drain), drip systems, and aeroponics. Each of these systems can be more suited to certain types of plants, and have different requirements in terms of complexity, cost, and maintenance.

Benefits of Hydroponics: Hydroponics is an efficient and sustainable method of gardening. It allows for faster plant growth, higher yields, and uses considerably less water than traditional soil gardening. It also eliminates the risk of soil-borne diseases and pests.

Challenges: Hydroponic gardening involves a learning curve. You'll need to closely monitor nutrient levels, pH balance, and water quality. Also, the initial setup can be more expensive than traditional gardening, although operational costs may be lower over time.

2. Diving Into Aquaponics
Aquaponics takes the hydroponics system a step further by adding fish into the equation. In an aquaponics system, fish and plants grow together in one integrated system. The fish waste provides an organic food source for the plants, and the plants naturally filter the water for the fish.

Components of an Aquaponic System: An aquaponic system is composed of a fish tank, a grow bed for the plants, and a small pump to move water between the two. The fish produce waste, bacteria in the system convert this waste into nutrients, and the plants absorb these nutrients, cleaning the water for the fish.

Choosing the Right Fish: The choice of fish for an aquaponic system depends on your local climate, the size of your system, and your goals (whether you want to eat the fish or just use them for their nutrient production). Tilapia, goldfish, and koi are popular choices for beginners.

Benefits of Aquaponics: Aquaponics shares many of the benefits of hydroponics. In addition, it offers the chance to raise fish, either for consumption or simply as pets. It also creates a balanced ecosystem that requires less intervention once it's well established.

Challenges: Setting up an aquaponics system can be complex and requires an understanding of both plant and fish care. It can also be more expensive to set up than a traditional garden or a basic hydroponics system.

Hydroponics and aquaponics offer exciting and innovative ways to expand your urban gardening repertoire. While they do present some challenges, the rewards they offer in terms of yield, efficiency, and sustainability make them worth exploring for the ambitious urban gardener.

Joining Urban Gardening Communities

Although this is similar in some ways to the previous section on "Engaging the Community in Urban Gardening", this section is fundamentally different in its approach in so much as here we talk about you as an individual joining pre-existing gardening communities.

Gardening can be an enriching solitary endeavor, providing a space for introspection and personal growth. However, it can also be a rewarding and enriching community activity.

Joining urban gardening communities can provide a platform for shared learning, mutual support, and collective action towards a greener city.

1. Types of Urban Gardening Communities

Urban gardening communities can take various forms, from informal networks of neighbors sharing gardening tips over the fence, to more structured groups with regular meetings and organized activities. Here are a few types to consider:

Community Gardens: These are shared spaces where people come together to grow food, flowers, or other plants. Community gardens often have individual plots for members, as well as shared areas like compost heaps or tool sheds.

Gardening Clubs and Societies: These groups often focus on specific aspects of gardening, such as growing roses or practicing organic methods. They usually meet regularly for talks, demonstrations, plant swaps, or visits to members' gardens.

Online Communities: Online platforms like forums, social media groups, and gardening apps can connect you with urban gardeners from around the world. These communities can offer a wealth of information and advice, accessible at any time.

2. Benefits of Joining Urban Gardening Communities

Joining an urban gardening community can bring multiple benefits.

Shared Knowledge and Experience: Every gardener has their own set of experiences and wisdom to share. Being part of a community allows you to learn from others and share your own knowledge, accelerating your learning curve and helping you tackle challenges more effectively.

Support and Encouragement: Gardening has its ups and downs. A supportive community can provide encouragement during tough times, celebrate your successes, and offer practical help when needed.

Resource Sharing: Communities often share resources, from spare seeds and cuttings to tools and compost. This can save you money and reduce waste, while also encouraging diversity in your garden.

Collective Action: Urban gardening communities can work together to advocate for green issues, from protecting local green spaces to campaigning for more allotment plots. There is power in numbers, and a community can have a significant impact.

3. How to Join Urban Gardening Communities

Joining an urban gardening community can be as simple as striking up a conversation with a fellow gardener at the local plant nursery, or signing up to an online gardening forum.
Research what's available in your area - look out for notice boards in parks or community centers, check your local council or library website, or search online. And remember, if you can't find a community that fits your needs, you could always start your own!

Joining an urban gardening community can bring a new dimension to your gardening journey. It offers an opportunity to connect with like-minded people, share in the joys and challenges of gardening, and contribute to a greener, healthier city.

Whether you're a novice or a seasoned gardener, there's a place for you in the thriving world of urban gardening communities.

Chapter 11: Conclusion: The Future of Urban Gardening and Sustainable Living

The Role of Urban Gardening in Sustainable Cities

As we draw to a close, it seems appropriate to take a look at the horizon. What is the future of urban gardening? How will it fit into the sustainability narrative that is increasingly shaping our cities, societies, and lives? As the world keeps turning, so too does our understanding of our relationship with our planet. And urban gardening, my friends, stands at the very heart of this evolving relationship.

Today, the world has more than 4 billion urban inhabitants, a figure projected to rise exponentially in the coming decades. But where does urban gardening fit into this picture? Therein lies our journey today.

The Role of Urban Gardening in Sustainable Cities

The advent of urban gardening was a response to the dilemma of high-density living, where open green spaces are a luxury rather than the norm. The human craving for connection with nature is intrinsic and compelling, and urban gardening provided an accessible, practical answer.

We've discussed the varied forms of urban gardening throughout this guide, from container gardens perched on high-rise balconies to sprawling community plots tucked between city buildings. But let's delve a little deeper into its role in creating a sustainable city.

Cities: From Concrete Jungles to Urban Forests

As urban populations grow, so too does the urban footprint, often at the expense of natural landscapes. But an increasing number of urban planners, architects, and city-dwellers are reimagining these concrete jungles, envisaging green, verdant spaces that balance urban life with nature.

Urban gardening is central to this vision. Not only does it provide an opportunity for city-dwellers to reconnect with nature and produce their own food, but it also offers environmental benefits that go far beyond the individual gardener.

For instance, urban gardens act as mini carbon sinks, helping to offset some of the carbon dioxide emissions in our cities. They also help to reduce urban heat islands – a phenomenon where cities are significantly warmer than surrounding rural areas. How? Plants, my friend, have this incredible ability to lower temperatures through a process called transpiration.

Urban gardens also play a vital role in biodiversity. Each patch of green in the city, no matter how small, provides a habitat for a wide variety of insects, birds, and small animals. This increase in biodiversity leads to a healthier and more balanced urban ecosystem, which can help improve the overall wellbeing of city dwellers.

The Role of Food Security in Urban Sustainability

At its core, urban gardening is about growing food – about turning underutilised spaces into productive ones. With the world's population booming and the climate changing, food security is a growing concern. Urban gardening can play a critical role in addressing this issue, particularly in cities where access to fresh, affordable produce can be a challenge.

As more individuals and communities turn to urban gardening, cities can become more self-sufficient, reducing their reliance on imported food and its associated carbon footprint. In this sense, urban gardening contributes to a more circular economy, where resources are used and reused locally, reducing waste and environmental impact.

The Importance of Education and Community Engagement

The transformative power of urban gardening is also seen in the hearts and minds of the people it touches. It's a wonderful, hands-on way to educate both children and adults about where food comes from, about the importance of healthy eating, and about the value of nature and biodiversity. It fosters a sense of community, bringing together people of all ages, backgrounds, and walks of life.

Community gardens, in particular, are hubs of social interaction and mutual aid. They can bring a community together, teach valuable skills, and foster a shared sense of responsibility towards our environment.

Promoting Wellness and Quality of Life

We can't talk about the future of urban gardening without discussing its immense health benefits. Gardening is a holistic practice, impacting us physically, mentally, and emotionally. The very act of planting and caring for a garden encourages physical activity, exposes us to sunlight (hello, vitamin D!), and even contributes to a healthier diet as we consume what we've grown.

On the mental health front, numerous studies have shown that gardening can reduce stress, anxiety, and depression. The practice of tending to plants, watching them grow and flourish, gives a sense of achievement, purpose, and connection to something larger than ourselves. This profound impact on our well-being, combined with the societal benefits of urban gardening, makes it a powerful tool for improving overall quality of life in our cities.

Urban Gardening and Technological Innovation

Looking ahead, technology is set to play an increasingly important role in urban gardening. From smart watering systems that conserve water to vertical gardening solutions that optimize space, technology is making it easier and more efficient to garden in urban environments.

Urban farms of the future might even incorporate elements of indoor farming, hydroponics, and aquaponics, harnessing cutting-edge technology to grow food in entirely new ways. These advancements will not only make urban gardening more accessible but also increase its potential output, contributing to city-wide sustainability efforts.

Policy Support and Infrastructure Development

The future of urban gardening also hinges on the support it receives from local governments and institutions. Policies that encourage urban gardening, such as the provision of community garden spaces, educational programs, and financial incentives, will play a crucial role in promoting this practice.

Similarly, the development of green infrastructure – incorporating vegetation and green spaces into urban design – is key. From green roofs and walls to the creation of 'edible landscapes' in public parks, the possibilities are exciting and nearly limitless.

As we look to the future, it's clear that urban gardening has a central role to play in the sustainable cities of tomorrow. Through the cultivation of green spaces, we can not only improve our personal well-being but also contribute to larger sustainability goals, such as reducing carbon emissions, increasing biodiversity, and enhancing food security.

While the challenges of urban living continue to evolve, so too do the solutions. Urban gardening is a testament to our ability to adapt, innovate, and find harmony with nature, even amidst concrete and skyscrapers.

Let's continue to cultivate this green revolution in our cities, nurturing our urban gardens as they, in turn, nurture us. The journey of sustainable living is a lifelong one, and it's one we're all taking together. Here's to greener, healthier, and more vibrant cities of the future. And remember, every plant counts!

The Growing Trend of Urban Farming

In the midst of the concrete and steel of our cities, an unexpected trend has taken root – urban farming. It's a movement that's been gaining momentum, driven by an increasingly urban global population, concern for the environment, and the desire for fresh, locally-sourced food. Let's dive a little deeper into this flourishing trend.

The Resurgence of a Basic Need

As humanity transitioned from agrarian societies to industrial and now digital ones, many of us have become removed from our food sources. We've grown used to walking into a supermarket and finding an array of produce available, often without thinking about how it got there. Yet, a growing number of urban dwellers are reconnecting with the land—or, in this case, the land tucked amidst the city blocks. They're tilling soil, planting seeds, and reaping harvests, all within the city limits.

This isn't just about fresh tomatoes or crisp lettuces. This is about rediscovering the joy and satisfaction that comes from growing your own food. It's about understanding the cycles of nature, the rhythm of the seasons, and the miracle that is a tiny seed transforming into something you can eat. This, in essence, is the soul of the urban farming movement.

From Vacant Lots to Vibrant Farms

One of the most inspiring aspects of urban farming is its innovative use of space. As we've explored, city dwellers have been creative in their quest to farm, transforming vacant lots, rooftops, balconies, and even walls into green, productive spaces.

The transformation of these often neglected spaces is about more than just aesthetics. These urban farms are improving air quality, reducing runoff, providing habitat for local wildlife, and of course, producing food. It's an incredible example of how we can transform our urban landscapes to be more sustainable and resilient.

Urban Farms: A Source of Local, Sustainable Produce

A significant advantage of urban farming is the opportunity to source food locally. Transporting food from farm to table often involves a significant amount of carbon emissions, particularly if the food is traveling long distances. By growing food in the city, urban farms can help to drastically cut this food mileage, contributing to a reduction in greenhouse gas emissions.

Moreover, because the produce is grown and sold locally, it's often fresher and tastier. Have you ever tasted a tomato that's just been picked from the vine? It's a world of difference from one that's been sitting in a truck or on a store shelf.

Additionally, urban farms often employ sustainable farming practices, such as composting, water conservation, and organic methods, further enhancing their environmental credentials.

Empowering Communities Through Urban Farming

Urban farms often serve as much more than just a source of food—they can be the heart of a community. Community-based urban farms are particularly powerful, serving as spaces where individuals can come together to learn, share, and connect with each other and the environment.

These urban farms can become educational hubs, teaching people of all ages about agriculture, nutrition, and sustainability. They can help to address issues of food security, providing access to fresh, affordable produce in areas that might not otherwise have it. They can even provide jobs and training opportunities, contributing to local economies.

Urban Farming: A Growing Field

The field of urban farming is ripe with potential, and as we look to the future, it's clear that this trend is more than just a passing fad. As our cities continue to grow, and our planet continues to face environmental challenges, urban farming will play an increasingly vital role in creating sustainable, resilient cities.

From microgreens grown in vertical farms to honey produced in rooftop apiaries, the possibilities are as diverse as our cities themselves. Urban farming represents a marriage of the old and the new, as traditional farming techniques meet modern innovation, all within the urban landscape.

Technological Innovations in Urban Farming

Urban farming is a field ripe for innovation, and already we're seeing some incredible advancements. From hydroponics and aquaponics to vertical farming systems, technology is enabling us to grow more food in less space, often with less water and fewer chemicals.

Take vertical farming, for instance. This method allows for the cultivation of plants in vertically stacked layers or inclined surfaces, often within controlled environments. This means food can be grown year-round, regardless of the weather, and without the need for soil. It's an exciting prospect for space-starved cities, and we're likely to see more of these systems in the years to come.

Similarly, hydroponics and aquaponics (the combination of fish farming with plant cultivation) are water-wise solutions that could redefine what's possible in urban agriculture. They allow for the efficient use of resources, making them well-suited to the constraints of city environments.

Policy and Urban Farming

The rise of urban farming has not gone unnoticed by policy-makers. In many cities around the world, local governments are starting to recognize the multiple benefits that urban farming can bring, and are implementing policies to support its development.

These range from zoning regulations that allow for urban agriculture, to funding and resources for community farming projects, to educational programs in schools. These policy supports are crucial for nurturing the growth of urban farming and ensuring that its benefits can be accessed by all city residents, not just a privileged few.

Looking Forward

Urban farming is a movement rooted in respect - respect for our food, for our communities, and for our planet. As this trend continues to grow, it has the potential to transform our cities, making them greener, more sustainable, and more connected places.

But perhaps most importantly, urban farming brings us back to a fundamental relationship - the one between us and the food we eat. It's a reminder of the cycles of life, of the joy of watching something grow, of the satisfaction of a home-cooked meal made with ingredients you've grown yourself. And it's a chance to share these experiences with our neighbors, our friends, our families.

The growing trend of urban farming is a beacon of change and a sign of a future where sustainability and urban living go hand in hand. It's a testament to our ability to innovate, adapt, and create, even in the most unlikely of places. So, here's to the urban farmers, the green-thumbed city-dwellers, the pioneers of this urban agricultural revolution. Let's keep sowing the seeds of change.

Lessons from Urban Gardening Experts

The world of urban gardening is rich with knowledge, shared through the trials, errors, and successes of countless city-dwelling green thumbs. Let's delve into some invaluable lessons from urban gardening experts that can help guide your journey.

Start Small, Dream Big

One piece of advice that many experienced urban gardeners share is to start small. You don't need a massive rooftop garden or an expansive community plot to begin. A few pots on a balcony, a window sill herb garden, or even a single indoor plant is a great place to start.
Starting small allows you to learn the basics without feeling overwhelmed. It's easier to understand the needs of a few plants than a large variety. As your confidence and skills grow, so can your garden.

Yet, while starting small, always dream big. Envision what you want your urban garden to become. Do you see a lush balcony filled with flowers and herbs? A productive vegetable garden? Or a peaceful green oasis? Let your vision inspire and guide you.

Understand Your Environment

Successful urban gardening requires a deep understanding of your specific urban environment. Every city, every neighborhood, every building has its own microclimate. An experienced urban gardener learns to work with, not against, these unique conditions.

Do you get full sun, or is your space mostly shaded? Do you have a lot of space, or just a small balcony? Are there certain pests or challenges you need to contend with? Understanding these factors will guide you in choosing the right plants and gardening techniques.

Choose the Right Plants

Not every plant is suited for the urban environment. Some plants thrive in small spaces, others need room to spread. Some can handle pollution, wind, or the heat radiated from buildings, while others cannot.

The experts recommend choosing plants that are well-suited to your specific conditions. Do your research, ask for advice, and learn from experience. And remember, choosing native plants or plants adapted to your local climate will often yield the best results.

Maximize Your Space

Urban gardeners become masters at making the most of the space they have. This might involve using vertical space by installing wall planters or trellises, using hanging pots, or simply arranging plants strategically.

This is where creativity comes in. Your urban garden is not just a place to grow food or flowers—it's also an opportunity to create a beautiful, personal space that brings you joy.

Care for Your Soil

In the city, good soil can be hard to come by. Yet, healthy soil is crucial for a successful garden. Many urban gardening experts recommend using quality potting soil and regularly adding organic matter, such as compost, to keep it nutrient-rich.

If you're gardening in the ground, you may also want to test your soil for contaminants—something that's unfortunately common in urban areas. Safe, healthy soil is the foundation of a thriving garden.

Learn from Each Season

Every season is a learning opportunity. Pay attention to how your plants respond to different conditions throughout the year. What thrives in the spring may struggle in the heat of summer, and what grows well one year might not the next. The more you observe and learn from each season, the more attuned you'll become to the rhythms of nature, even in the heart of the city.

Connect with Your Community

Urban gardening is a wonderful way to connect with your community. Whether it's sharing your harvest with neighbors, trading tips with other urban gardeners, or joining a community garden, these connections can enrich your urban gardening experience.

In the end, one of the most essential lessons from urban gardening experts is that gardening is a journey. There will be challenges and setbacks, but also many rewards—from the taste of a homegrown tomato to the buzz of a bee visiting your flowers, or the simple joy of seeing a seed sprout. Embrace this journey with patience, curiosity, and a willingness to learn and you, too, can become an expert in your own urban garden.

Building Resilience

Experts in the field stress the importance of resilience in urban gardening. Plants may succumb to disease, pests may invade, and adverse weather may wreak havoc. But these are all parts of the process. Do not be disheartened. Learn from these experiences and use them to grow stronger and smarter.

Resilience also applies to your garden's ecosystem. Building a garden that can withstand changes in weather, resist pests, and regenerate soil is a lesson in creating resilience in our own lives.

Nurturing Relationships

Many expert urban gardeners highlight the importance of relationships - with the land, the plants, the local ecosystem, and the broader community. The way you tend to your garden is a reflection of these relationships.

Remember, gardening isn't just about producing food or beautifying spaces; it's about cultivating relationships. Cherishing these relationships nurtures a deep respect for the interconnectedness of life.

Closing Thoughts

The lessons from urban gardening experts provide us with a roadmap, full of practical advice and hard-earned wisdom. They remind us that while every garden is unique, the fundamental principles of gardening hold true whether you're farming in the countryside or tending to a single pot in the heart of the city.

They also remind us of the broader impacts of our urban gardening endeavors. How it links us to the cycles of nature, contributes to the well-being of our urban communities, and moves us towards a more sustainable future.

So, as you continue your journey as an urban garder, keep these lessons close. Draw on them for guidance, inspiration, and reassurance. Remember, every urban gardener was once a beginner, and every expert is still learning.

How Urban Gardening is Changing Cities

Urban gardening is not just about producing food or creating green spaces—it's a transformative movement that is reshaping our cities in remarkable ways. From rooftops to roadside patches, unused lots to vertical walls, the concrete jungles are gradually turning green, one garden at a time. Let's explore the ways in which urban gardening is changing the face and feel of our cities.

Improving Food Security and Nutrition

One of the most direct impacts of urban gardening is improved food security. In many cities, especially in underserved neighborhoods, access to fresh, nutritious food can be a challenge. Urban gardens, however, are turning this around.

From community gardens providing fresh produce to local families, to entrepreneurial urban farms selling their harvest at city farmer's markets, urban gardening is playing a significant role in reducing 'food deserts'. This movement not only ensures better access to fresh produce but also fosters nutritional awareness among city dwellers.

Enhancing Community Engagement

Urban gardening is also fostering community engagement and cohesion. Community gardens are becoming spaces where people from different walks of life come together, interact, share, and learn from each other. These gardens are not just about growing plants—they're about cultivating relationships, bridging generational and cultural divides, and fostering a sense of belonging.

In addition, these communal green spaces are often involved in educational initiatives, teaching children and adults alike about gardening, sustainability, and the importance of healthy eating. This community-led model of education can have profound impacts on neighborhoods, instilling a sense of stewardship and shared responsibility for the environment.

Reducing Urban Heat and Improving Air Quality

Urban gardens are playing a crucial role in mitigating some of the environmental challenges cities face. Concrete and asphalt absorb heat, making cities significantly warmer than surrounding rural areas—a phenomenon known as the 'urban heat island effect.' Plants, however, cool the air through a process known as transpiration. As a result, areas with urban gardens can be noticeably cooler.

In addition, plants absorb carbon dioxide and pollutants, improving air quality. They also increase humidity and reduce dust, making cities healthier and more comfortable places to live.

Creating Green Spaces and Enhancing Biodiversity

In many cities, green spaces are few and far between. Urban gardening is changing this, transforming underused and neglected areas into vibrant, green havens. These spaces provide a much-needed connection to nature for city dwellers, improving mental health and overall wellbeing.

Urban gardens can also play a role in supporting biodiversity. By providing habitats for a variety of insects, birds, and other wildlife, urban gardens can contribute to the health and resilience of local ecosystems. This is particularly important in cities, which often lack diverse natural habitats.

Promoting Sustainability

Urban gardening is at the forefront of the sustainability movement in cities. It encourages local food production, reducing the carbon footprint associated with transporting food over long distances. It also promotes sustainable practices, such as composting and water conservation.

Furthermore, urban gardening can play a role in waste reduction, as city dwellers find that composting their green waste is a productive use of materials that would otherwise go to landfill.

Urban Gardening: The Future of Our Cities

Urban gardening is not a passing trend—it's a powerful and transformative movement. It's creating healthier, more sustainable, and more resilient cities. It's bringing communities together and fostering a deep connection with the natural world. It's a response to some of the most pressing challenges we face today—from food security to climate change—and a manifestation of our innate desire to nurture, grow, and create.

As we look to the future, it's clear that urban gardening will continue to play a vital role in shaping our cities. It represents a new paradigm of urban living—one that embraces the coexistence of nature and urban development, recognizes the importance of community, and values sustainability.

Innovative Urban Design

Urban gardening is inspiring innovative urban design that integrates green spaces into city living. The notion of 'green infrastructure' is gaining traction. This concept weaves natural elements into the cityscape, creating a blend of natural and built environments. Urban farms on rooftops, vertical gardens on building facades, and green corridors along streets are all part of this vision.

Changing Policy Landscape

The rise of urban gardening is also influencing policies. City governments are starting to recognize the myriad benefits of urban gardens and are adapting urban planning and zoning regulations accordingly. Supportive policies are emerging, from providing resources for community gardens to establishing urban agriculture programs.

Growing Economy

Urban gardening is also spurring economic growth. It's generating local jobs, supporting small businesses, and stimulating local economies. From urban farms selling produce to restaurants and markets, to businesses offering urban gardening supplies or services, this green revolution is creating new economic opportunities in the heart of our cities.

Engaging Youth

Urban gardening is engaging the younger generation, teaching them the importance of nature, the value of hard work, and the satisfaction of growing their own food. Schools are incorporating gardening programs, which not only provide a hands-on learning experience but also help instill a sense of responsibility and pride in the students.

Instilling Hope

Perhaps most importantly, urban gardening instills hope. It's a tangible action that individuals and communities can take to make a difference. It demonstrates that it's possible to live in a city and still have a deep, meaningful connection with nature. It shows that each one of us can contribute to a greener, healthier, and more sustainable future.

In the face of daunting global challenges, urban gardening is a testament to human ingenuity, resilience, and our profound need for connection—with each other, with our food, and with the natural world. It's a testament to the power of small actions and the ripple effects they can have.

So, as we envision the future of our cities, let's envision them greener and more vibrant, filled with gardens and the life they support. Let's envision them as places where people gather to grow, learn, share, and celebrate the simple, beautiful act of tending to a garden. Because that's the power of urban gardening—it's not just changing our cities, it's changing us.

Final Thoughts

As we conclude our journey through the world of urban gardening in this book, I hope it has been as enlightening for you as it has been a pleasure for me to guide you through. Urban gardening is so much more than a hobby—it is a revolutionary act, an environmental solution, a community builder, and a path to personal wellness.

Reflecting on everything we've explored, it's clear that the act of urban gardening, of turning tiny urban spaces into thriving green spots, represents a potent symbol of resilience, hope, and sustainability in our concrete jungles. It exemplifies how we, as humans, have the remarkable ability to adapt and to make our surroundings better, healthier, and more sustainable.

The beauty of urban gardening is in its accessibility. It doesn't matter how much space you have or how green your thumb is—everyone can participate. You can start small, even with a single plant, and that in itself is a significant step. Remember, every garden started from a single seed.

From learning about the role of urban gardening in sustainable cities, to understanding the growing trend of urban farming, embarking on your journey as an urban gardener, gaining wisdom from experts, and realizing the transformative impact of urban gardening on cities—we have covered significant ground.

Use this knowledge to spur you into action, to start or continue your urban gardening journey with a renewed sense of purpose and inspiration.

As you go ahead, remember that every urban garden, irrespective of its size, is a step towards a greener city. Every plant you nurture, every bit of compost you make, every new gardening skill you acquire contributes to the larger picture—a sustainable, resilient city that harmoniously merges the natural and built environments.

It's clear that urban gardening is not just a trend—it's a movement, a revolution. It's a testament to our ability to adapt, innovate, and reimagine our relationship with nature. Urban gardening is transforming our cities, making them healthier, greener, and more livable.

But beyond these tangible benefits, urban gardening offers something perhaps even more important: a connection. In the heart of the city, amid the concrete and glass, a garden connects us to the rhythms of nature, to the joy of watching something grow, to the satisfaction of nurturing life. It connects us to our communities, to our neighbors, and to ourselves.

So, let us embrace urban gardening, not just as a pastime, but as a path towards a sustainable, vibrant, and green future.

Let's fill our cities with gardens, our lives with greenery, and our hearts with the joy and satisfaction that comes from tending to a piece of this Earth. Because ultimately, we are not just growing plants—we are growing a better, greener, and more sustainable future for us all.

In the end, the future of urban gardening is indeed promising and vibrant. And remember, the future of urban gardening is not just in the hands of the experts, or the policymakers, or the urban farmers—it's also in your hands.

So, go ahead, get your hands dirty, nurture that green thumb, and become a part of this incredible journey being made by truly remarkable people... the journey into the wonderful world of urban gardening.

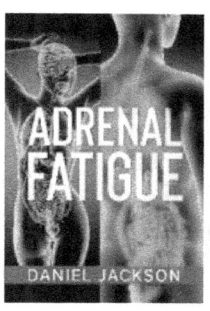   

Take a look at more great books available from Rockwood Publishing

... **some for FREE!**

Just visit the link below:

rockwoodpublishing.co.uk

Published by Rockwood Publishing 2023

Copyright and Trademarks. This publication is Copyright 2023 by Rockwood Publishing. All products, publications, software and services mentioned and recommended in this publication are protected by trademarks. In such instances, all trademarks & copyright belong to the respective owners. All rights reserved. No part of this book may be reproduced or transferred in any form or by any means, graphic, electronic, or mechanical, including photocopying, recording, taping, or by any information storage retrieval system, without the written permission of the author. Pictures used in this book are either royalty free pictures bought from stock-photo websites or have the source mentioned underneath the picture.

Disclaimer and Legal Notice. This product is not legal or medical advice and should not be interpreted in that manner. You need to do your own due diligence to determine if the content of this product is right for you. The author and the affiliates of this product are not liable for any damages or losses associated with the content in this product. While every attempt has been made to verify the information shared in this publication, neither the author nor the affiliates assume any responsibility for errors, omissions or contrary interpretation of the subject matter herein. Any perceived slights to any specific person(s) or organisation(s) are purely unintentional. We have no control over the nature, content and availability of the websites listed in this book. The inclusion of any website links does not necessarily imply a recommendation or endorse the views expressed within them. Rockwood Publishing takes no responsibility for, and will not be liable for, the websites being temporarily unavailable or being removed from the Internet. The accuracy and completeness of information provided herein and opinions stated herein are not guaranteed or warranted to produce any particular results, and the advice and strategies contained herein may not be suitable for every individual. The author shall not be liable for any loss incurred as a consequence of the use and application, directly or indirectly, of any information presented in this work. This publication is designed to provide information in regards to the subject matter covered. The information included in this book has been compiled to give an overview of the subject(s) and detail some of the symptoms, treatments etc. that are available to people with this condition. It is not intended to give medical advice. For a firm diagnosis of your condition, and for a treatment plan suitable for you, you should consult your doctor or consultant. The writer of this book and the publisher are not responsible for any damages or negative consequences following any of the treatments or methods highlighted in this book. Website links are for informational purposes and should not be seen as a personal endorsement; the same applies to the products detailed in this book. The reader should also be aware that although the web links included were correct at the time of writing, they may become out of date in the future.

Disclaimers

The content contained within this book is for information and entertainment purposes only, and in no way purports to represent professional medical opinion. It should NOT be used as a substitute for expert advice, and you must consult with your designated health professional before acting upon any information contained herein or before undertaking any practice whose methodology is referred to in this book. The author is NOT a registered health professional and the text merely represents personal opinion, not medical fact. The author cannot be held responsible for the consequences of any action derived from the reading of this book, as the content is not based on diagnosis and subsequent regimen. It is the reader's responsibility to seek proper, professional medical advice from a registered health practitioner in connection with any material contained within this book.

Legal Disclaimer (part 1)

Nothing in this book should be construed as an attempt to diagnose, treat or cure. The information in this book is intended to be a community resource. The author takes no responsibility for any informational material or brochures produced using information taken from this book. The author has endeavoured to ensure that all information is correct at the time of publication. This information, however, is subject to change without notice. The author makes no warranty with regard to the accuracy of any information and will not be liable for any errors or omissions. Any liability that arises as a result of this information is hereby excluded to the fullest extent allowed by law.

This information should not be used as a substitute for seeking independent professional advice.

Legal Disclaimer (part 2)

Disclaimer and Terms of Use:

a) i. In publishing this information, the author makes no representations concerning the efficacy, appropriateness or suitability of any products or treatments. Use this information at your own risk. The compiler is not a doctor and has no medical background or training.

ii. Statements and information regarding dietary supplements, books and any products mentioned have not been evaluated by any health authority and are not intended to diagnose, treat, cure or prevent any disease or health condition.

b) In view of the possibility of human error, neither the author nor any other party involved in providing this information, warrant that the information contained therein is in every respect accurate or complete and they are not responsible nor liable for any errors or omissions that may be found or for the results obtained from the use of such information. The entire risk as to use of this information is assumed by the user.

c) You are encouraged to consult other sources and confirm the information.

d) The information you access is provided "as is". No warranty, expressed or implied, is given as to the accuracy, completeness or timeliness of any information herein, or for obtaining legal advice. To the fullest extent permissible pursuant to applicable law, neither the author nor any other parties who have been involved in the creation, preparation, printing, or delivering of this information assume responsibility for the completeness, accuracy, timeliness, errors or omissions of said information and assume no liability for any direct, incidental, consequential, indirect, or punitive damages as well as any circumstance for any complication, injuries, side effects or other medical accidents to person or property arising from or in connection with the use or reliance upon any information contained herein.

e) The author is not responsible for the contents of any linked site or any link contained in a linked site, or any changes or update to such sites. The inclusion of any link does not imply endorsement by the author. The author makes no representations or claims as to the quality, content and accuracy of the information, services, products, messages which may be provided by such resources, and specifically disclaims any warranties, including but not limited to implied or express warranties of merchantability or fitness for any particular usage, application or purpose.

f) The information provided is general in nature and is intended for educational and informational purposes only. It is not intended to replace or substitute the evaluation, judgment, diagnosis, and medical or preventative care of a physician, paediatrician, therapist and/or health care provider.

g) Any medical, nutritional, dietetic, therapeutic or other decisions, dosages, treatments or drug regimes should be made in consultation with a health care practitioner. Do not discontinue treatment or medication without first consulting your physician, clinician or therapist.

h) By reading this information, you signify your assent to these terms and conditions of use. If you do not agree to these terms and conditions of use, do not read/use this information. If any provision of these terms and conditions of use shall be determined to be unlawful, void or for any reason unenforceable, then that provision shall be deemed severable from this agreement and shall not affect the validity and enforceability of any remaining provisions.

i) The information, services, products, messages and other materials, individually and collectively, are provided with the understanding that the author is not engaged in rendering medical advice or recommendations.

j) The information and the terms of use are subject to change without notice. The material provided as is without warranty of any kind and may include inaccuracies and/or typographical errors. The author makes no representations about the suitability of this information for any purpose. The author disclaims all warranties with regard to this information, including all implied warranties, and in no event shall the author be held liable, resulting from, or in any way related to, the use of this information.

k) The unauthorized alteration of the content of this information is expressly prohibited. The author, its agents and representatives shall not be responsible for any claims, actions or damages which may arise on account of the unauthorized alteration of this information.

www.ingramcontent.com/pod-product-compliance
Lightning Source LLC
Chambersburg PA
CBHW070551010526
44118CB00012B/1289